MAKING
TROUSERS
for Men & Women

Creative Publishing international

First published in the United States of America by
Creative Publishing international, Inc., a member of
Quayside Publishing Group
400 First Avenue North
Suite 300
Minneapolis, MN 55401
1-800-328-3895
www.creativepub.com

ISBN-13: 978-1-58923-449-9
ISBN-10: 1-58923-449-9

10 9 8 7 6 5 4 3 2 1

Library of Congress Cataloging-in-Publication Data

Coffin, David Page.
  Making trousers for men and women : a multimedia sewing workshop / David Coffin.
    p. cm.
  Includes index.
  ISBN-13: 978-1-58923-449-9
  ISBN-10: 1-58923-449-9
  1. Pants. 2. Men's clothing. 3. Women's clothing. I. Title.

TT605.C65 2009
646'.3--dc22

2009011156

Technical Editor: Carol Fresia
Copy Editor: Nancy Chute
Proofreader: Karen Ruth
Cover & Book Design: Kathie Alexander
Page Layout: Silke Braun
Fashion Ilustrations: Maite Lafuente

Printed in Singapore

MAKING
TROUSERS

for Men & Women

A MULTIMEDIA SEWING WORKSHOP
David Page Coffin

Creative Publishing
international

CONTENTS

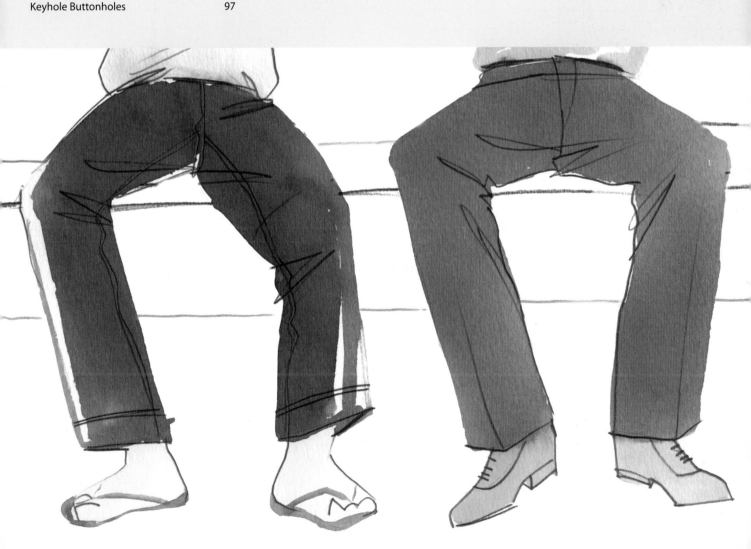

HOW TO USE THIS BOOK AND COMPANION DVD

Greetings, and thanks for taking a look at my book! Before you flip to whatever the chase is for you on your pants-making journey, I hope you'll read the introduction and Chapter 1, which is a tour of custom-made and ready-to-wear pants. This tour is my effort to bring readers to a common point of pants literacy. We'll take a close look at selected samples from the trousers universe, and you'll learn which elements I felt were interesting enough to demonstrate and to discuss in more detail throughout the rest of the book.

This book also includes a DVD-ROM, designed for viewing on a computer, not in a DVD player. Its primary purpose is to give you video demonstrations of all the techniques in the book. I've also included many more things that simply wouldn't fit in the book—new ideas, more and bigger pictures from my collection of tour garments and pants I've made, plus clickable versions of the Sources and Further Reading sections, and links to some neat blogs and forums that I thought pants makers would be likely to enjoy.

The video content evolved from simple demos of the described techniques into something much more like a complete video workshop on how to expand and vary the techniques in the book. I filmed the videos while preparing the sample garments, playing a bit with each of the techniques, so I wanted to share that process and those results with you, too. The video material on the DVD—which contains about 2 hours' worth of clips—not only demonstrates the techniques described in the book, it also covers new material only alluded to in the text or not mentioned at all. (Review the list of contents on page 136 and on the DVD itself.)

The DVD is definitely a valuable companion to have running while reading the book. Its onscreen photo galleries also provide more than 180 additional photos of garment details. You'll also find it contains a few full-size, printable patterns for details that I use on my own pants. Feel free to adapt them to suit your purposes.

For more information, discussion, and book-related extras, visit http://makingtrouserswithdpc.blogspot.com, my blog all about making trousers and specifically designed for the readers of this book.

I hope you find this multimedia workshop fun and useful as you make your journey!

BEYOND FIT AND STYLE

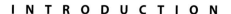

My very first sewn garment was a pair of pants. They didn't really fit (I'd used an unaltered Vogue pattern), they were too hot, and the pockets were too big and in the wrong place—but they were exactly the pants I'd wanted: made of tweed, lined in cotton sateen, with no belt loops, and with all-cotton pockets and a little pouch for my Swiss Army knife. I LOVED them! The main problem was that I had no idea how to create a second pair. My class instructor just took over whenever I didn't know what to do next. She'd handled the tricky parts and, of course, I still needed to refine all those pattern-related issues. So, I turned my attention to something I thought would be easier. Shirts! Ha!

When I finally returned to pants fifteen or so years later, I had a better idea of how to proceed. Obviously, I needed a fitted basic pants pattern, and I didn't want to struggle over getting one. As you'll learn, I found a solution to that problem and was soon ready to hit the books, always my primary resource when undertaking new ventures. (You'll find an annotated listing of my favorite pants books on page 134.)

My most significant first step was to drag out the few men's and women's study pants I'd collected over the years to examine their construction and details. (You'll get a good look at them in Chapter 1.) I knew that I would eventually make another pair of pants, so I was collecting interesting specimens to plunder. What exactly was I collecting? It didn't matter to me if they fit well, or even if I could wear them, or if they were generally in a style I liked. I wasn't planning on copying any of these garments entirely. The deciding factor was always in the details, either hidden deep inside the construction or visible on the surface. These compelling features are exactly the focus of this book: the details and the construction methods, not the fit or the style. All the details and construction ideas I have included can be applied to any style of pants and don't have much, if any, impact on the fit.

ON NOT FITTING PANTS

If I learned anything from my shirtmaking years, it was that fitting is a huge challenge that can easily eat up all your available sewing time and block all further sewing progress, if you let it. It also seemed that even apparently minor fitting problems could continue to resist solution if you didn't have a pretty comprehensive understanding of all the issues that could be involved. Because I'd never wanted to sew for anyone but myself and a few loved ones, I saw no reason to become learned in these issues. If someone offered to provide me with a well-fitting, basic pants pattern or two so I could get on with the good stuff, I'd be delighted! Well, it turns out there are a lot of skillful people who can provide that service, from local dressmakers or tailors to nationally recognized fitting specialists and sewing authorities.

My personal solution was to order a custom pants pattern draft by mail, using a measurement chart and posture questionnaire from Stanley Hostek, a wonderful and long-retired tailoring teacher who still offers a pants-drafting service. I'd also been lucky enough to have a muslin-draping session with a fitting expert I'd met while editing her article on pants-fitting for *Threads* magazine. By combining the best-working parts from both of the resulting patterns (they were remarkably similar) and tweaking my way through a simple muslin trial, I was in business. Moral of story: Pick your battles!

If you do want to become the pants-fitting guru in your neighborhood, you'll need to test your skills on a LOT of bodies, but you'll have plenty of help. There's no more popular topic in the sewing literature than fitting, and pants are the number-one problem garment. Based on my experience as editor for many an article on this painful subject, I'd personally gravitate toward drafting a basic pants pattern, either by hand or with a computer, as the first step to achieving a usable

"The deciding factor was always in the details, either hidden deep inside the construction or visible on the surface."

pattern (rather than trying to alter an existing commercial pattern). Even drafts, however, must be tested in muslin to reveal postural, weight distribution, and silhouette issues that aren't easily captured in measurements.

The logic of drafting pants from a well-fitting skirt is compelling. If you have at least one straight skirt that fits reasonably well above the hips, your pants-fitting work from waist to hips may, for the most part, be already done. The most significant aid I've had in my own fitting efforts has been a cast body form, created by wrapping one's own body in plaster, duct tape, or something similar, to copy its exact contours. Once you get over the inevitable shock of seeing your own shape as others do, the benefits of working directly on yourself will amaze you. The form I use started with a plaster-bandage cast filled with self-hardening foam, and it's still serving me well after at least a dozen years. My cast form is not designed for pants, and I've not used it for fitting below the waist, but many people swear by their custom-made pants forms. I see no advantage to fitting on a standard body or pants form that has not been customized—unless you're designing ready-to-wear. (See the DVD links for pants-drafting and custom form-making resources.)

Finally, I'd like to point out that the more closely any garment fits, the harder it is to make that fit work—unless you're using swimsuit fabric! So don't underestimate the power of simply adding back a little ease if you're struggling to achieve a graceful fit. This approach is especially true when fitting the critical areas of the crotch curve, hips, and seat, none of which is traditionally close-fitting in tailored trousers, either for men or for women. Long, vertical drape lines are always preferable to short, diagonal or horizontal stress lines, at least to my eye.

ON NOT BEING A PRO

I'm an amateur, not a professional, garment maker—and unapologetically so. And, because it's for my fellow amateurs that I'm writing this book, not for aspiring professionals or manufacturers, I'd like to briefly explore some of the more interesting implications of this distinction.

Being an amateur means that, however much I'm committed to high-quality results, I'm not primarily interested in efficiency, standard practices, economy, or any other profit- or production-oriented constraints that affect working sewers. I'm primarily interested in enjoying my sewing time, and that's what guides me as I gather and develop techniques. Obviously, I want great results, but I also want to indulge my preferences for experimentation, for not doing things the same way every time, and for making each new project a chance to try out a new idea, fabric, detail, or style. I enjoy being free to take risks, to try out hare-brained schemes and have instructive failures, to take as long as I want to finish anything, and to not sew at all whenever other interests take priority. I'm my own quality-control examiner, and I happily regard my sewing skills as eternally in development. In short, I don't make products. I do projects.

This approach is very agreeable—in fact, it's the reason I continue to enjoy sewing—but there are downsides. For example, I'll never develop the amazing precision, the effortless control, or the speed of a sewer who makes the same garment, or part of a garment, dozens of times every day under constant scrutiny. Any process that requires the practice and precision that only an all-day, every-day sewing professional can provide is both out of my range and also not covered in this book.

Rest assured, then, that all the techniques presented in this workshop require only care and patience to apply at least as effectively as I've managed to. I have not tested any of these techniques in a production or sales environment, simply because I've never worked in either. Any techniques that may have originated in a production environment, I'll be demonstrating as an amateur who has adapted them to his skills. I hope this fact will help make these techniques more accessible to other amateurs, without misrepresentation, but I do acknowledge that these methods might very well look different if they were demo'd by a master.

To any readers who would like to develop more than amateur skills and don't have a master handy to watch, I offer only two words: practice and commitment! If you were to make, say,

"I'm primarily interested in enjoying my sewing time, and that's what guides me as I gather and develop techniques."

fourteen pairs of pants, one right after the other, you'd learn far more, become much more efficient, develop new skills much faster, and probably wind up with a better-made fourteenth garment than if you made the same fourteen pairs over the course of the next several years, whenever you had the time. You can, however, certainly learn, improve, develop great skills, or make wonderful clothes that are as good as or better than the best production garments without such a marathon. Those of us who can't sew all day simply have to replace experience with patience, care, and a profound willingness to rip out and re-stitch all our not-quite-right seams!

Another downside is that I rarely have the luxury of making a test garment—let alone several—for every new project. Yet designers do this routinely. Most have full-time sample makers who test prospective designs multiple times, refining the pattern and zeroing in, by trial and error, on exactly the right techniques, fabrics, interfacings, and findings to make the design work. They're experienced enough to know that only testing will finally determine what goes best, and works best, with what. I do tests, too, but only on scraps and never as complete garments. So, ultimately, each garment I make reveals issues that I wish I'd known about before using up my last scrap of the fabric, and rarely do I get to apply that knowledge on a similar garment. It's just too boring to make the same thing over and over, and the fabric's gone anyway. So I learn much more slowly and never learn some things, I'm sure, at all.

Finally, there's the issue of the inside finish. Neat, elegant workmanship, inside and out, is definitely one of my aspirations as a sewer. Because I'm not sewing for customers, however, my projects only have to be ready for me, not for a showroom or for inspection by a critical client. Much as I like to admire other maker's garments, looking for unique details and polished sewn effects to plunder, I don't need to work up any signature features or brand-establishing finishes, worry about hanger appeal, or be concerned about consistency from one garment to another. I don't have to change my threads when I switch from garment topstitching to pocket finishing, or use matching fabrics for interior features that under normal circumstances only I will ever see. If it looks great on the outside, I'm happy. If I can indulge my inner patchworker with an odd scrap of contrasting fabric on the inside, I'm happier still.

If I wanted to make my garments more standardized, I'd start by developing fixed patterns and shaping or trimming templates for all those things that I instead improvise into shape when I get to them, such as fly linings and pocket bags. I'd buy a few interior fabrics by the bolt instead of digging through my scraps for unique combinations with each garment. And, I'd have to settle on one or two options for every detail that I now regard as totally subject to on-the-spot whimsy. It would be an interesting challenge and would require a lot of disciplined sample-making—but I'm pretty sure I wouldn't find it nearly as much fun as my own playful practices.

So, I'll largely leave all those extra interior-finish issues unexplored, except to reveal interior details in the many professionally made garments I've photographed for the book. Take from these examples what you will, set your own standards, and stick to them for as long as they make your sewing more satisfying and enjoyable.

CHAPTER ONE

LEARNING FROM CUSTOM AND READY-TO-WEAR GARMENTS

Examining interesting garments is to me an essential part of learning to sew. It's a great way to discover details and construction choices I want to emulate and it gives me a useful, real-world perspective that often challenges my assumptions about how things are supposed to be done. In short, it's a great way to develop my own garment-making standards.

If you're inspired to make clothes mostly by looking at existing garments, as I usually am, I'm sure you've observed that the methods and pattern pieces found in sewing patterns often don't provide exactly the details you've admired in ready-to-wear (RTW) or custom-made clothes. Figuring out how to recreate these details is a fascinating challenge, and it's usually more efficient than trying to find just the right instructions in a book or pattern.

So, before we talk about technique, let's examine a wide range of ready-to-wear and custom-made men's and women's traditional fly-fronted trousers, to see what we can learn from them. You'll soon realize that there's no single standard for quality, construction, or performance; nor is there only one good way to handle any pants-making process. I don't always find it worth the effort (or even possible!) to duplicate exactly what I find in high-

quality garments, but it's useful and inspiring to see the possibilities. We won't ignore the low end of the pants-making spectrum, because there are likely to be some clever, efficient ideas and techniques in there that we time- and skill-strapped home sewers can take advantage of.

At the outset, the main thing to note is that ALL of the garments in this tour are successful in their own ways. They didn't fall apart, they were comfortable, and they looked fine, so all are potentially worth plundering for techniques, details, and effects, whether we find these simply attractive or actually practical. They're here to offer us choices. (You'll find large photographs and even more sample garments on the companion DVD.)

I encourage you to make up your own mind about what you find worth emulating in these or any other garments. My hope is that from the detailed look I provide here, along with the techniques I describe in the construction chapters to come, you'll come away well informed about your pants-making options, and you'll have everything you need to make a wide variety of high-quality pants that will please YOU, whether you've got plenty of time to create a showpiece garment or you just want to whip up an everyday pair.

WHAT IS QUALITY CONSTRUCTION?

Years ago, the curator of a superb couture costume collection pointed out that two primary indications of quality construction in garments are the effort and time the maker was willing to expend in the pursuit of less bulk, thinner edges and more flexibility, and in making sure that transitions from thick to thin

are as imperceptible as possible. Take a look at the diagram on page 14 for a quick rundown of the main strategies for keeping seams and edges flat. Seam allowances pressed open are thinner than those pressed to one side, folded edges are thinner than seamed edges, and edges seamed to lining fabrics are thinner than those seamed to self-fabric.

My curator friend pointed to some very minimal overcasting and the lack of a lining inside a couture bustier, remarking how dramatically it disproved the home sewer's traditional conviction that well-made clothes must look as beautifully finished on the inside as on the outside. The main goals for inner construction are, simply, to keep the outside looking great and the overall thickness as minimal and supple as possible—even, if necessary, at the expense of what the garment looks like on the inside.

At the extreme of fashion, appearance obviously trumps practicality. But thinner, flatter, smoother, and more flexible edges and seams will generally wear less and be more comfortable, so it's clear that the principle is worth upholding even on sport and work clothing. Of course, priorities must always be balanced, so easier and faster will inevitably be factored against thin and flat—but, as a rule of thumb, going for thin is a very useful pointer toward quality, amply confirmed by the garments shown here.

SEAMS AND EDGES, FROM THIN TO THICK

A. Seam allowances, pressed open

B. Seam allowances, pressed to side

C. Edge folded

D. Edge lined

E. Self-fabric seam, allowances pressed open away from edge

F. Self-fabric seam, allowances pressed together at edge

■ Fashion fabric ■ Stitches ■ Lining fabric

TWO EXTREMES: L.L. BEAN JEANS AND YSL COUTURE

I'm starting with two garments—both traditional trousers—that are two ends of the spectrum, alpha and omega, bookends, in a way. This pair of women's cotton blue jeans from L.L. Bean sets a reasonable lower limit for serviceable pants construction and cost. The hand-stitched women's silk trousers made in the couture workrooms at the House of Yves Saint Laurent set a reasonable upper limit, both for construction and cost.

So, as you proceed on to the other garments in this tour, ask yourself: What additional features did these pants-makers add to their pants, and why did they add them, considering that L.L. Bean and YSL apparently concluded they were not necessary?

THE L.L. BEAN JEANS

The most interesting feature of this garment, to me, is all that isn't here. There are NO extras, nothing beyond the basics, with the exception of the little patch pocket inside the right-front scooped pocket and the back yokes, which replace darts, standard issue for jeans. There are two fronts, two backs, four—okay, five—pockets, a waistband with belt loops, and a zipper fly.

Note the self-fabric, unlined fly-shield layer (covering the zipper teeth), and unstiffened waistband. Throughout the garment, only the pocket is a different fabric. The waistband and the shield are each created by folding a single piece in half, so the pieces are not seamed at their outer edges. This technique creates a nice flat edge, but there are few other efforts toward thinness. The shield strip has been merely folded back, rather than trimmed, at the bottom to shape it (two layers become four). All fly pieces are seamed in, not cut on.

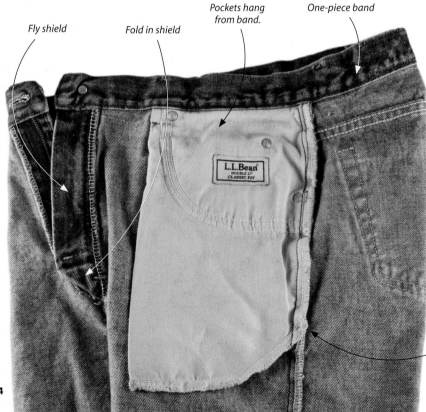

Fly shield

Fold in shield

Pockets hang from band.

One-piece band

L.L.Bean DOUBLE L CLASSIC FIT

Pocket and side seams are finished together.

All the pocket and garment side seam allowances are caught together with serging. Then they're pressed to the back and topstitched. All the remaining seams are flat-felled (wrapped together to one side and topstitched) or pressed to one side. The pocket bags extend up to, and hang from, the waistband.

THE YSL PANTS

This Yves Saint Laurent (YSL) garment has two fronts, two backs, two self-fabric pockets hanging from the waist, a shieldless zipper fly, and a waistband with belt loops, band filler, and band lining, plus three little fabric hanger loops. Again, there are no features beyond a slightly expanded version of the jeans list of utter basics for pants. Same basic formula as the jeans, but infinitely more care taken in the assembly. We'll take a closer look, because this is a surprisingly sophisticated garment despite its apparent simplicity. (Garment courtesy of Claire Shaeffer—thanks!)

Fly facings are cut on rather than seamed on (folds are thinner than seams), and the zipper is hand-stitched to the facings after the fly is formed.

The waistband is stitched to the pants, then wrapped around a woven grosgrain ribbon (called petersham) as reinforcement, and topstitched to the ribbon along every edge.

A lining fabric in matching but lighter-weight silk is hand-tacked to the band edges.

The hand-overcast side and inseam seam allowances are cut extra wide (approximately 1 inch [2.5 cm]) to add weight to their seams, helping them to drape more smoothly.

The pocket seam allowances are carefully butted and whipstitched, with no overlaps, to the side seam allowances, which are cut away when they reach the pocket. There is a total of three fabric layers at the pockets, no facings.

This YSL women's garment is an example of classic menswear styling, handmade with couture techniques.

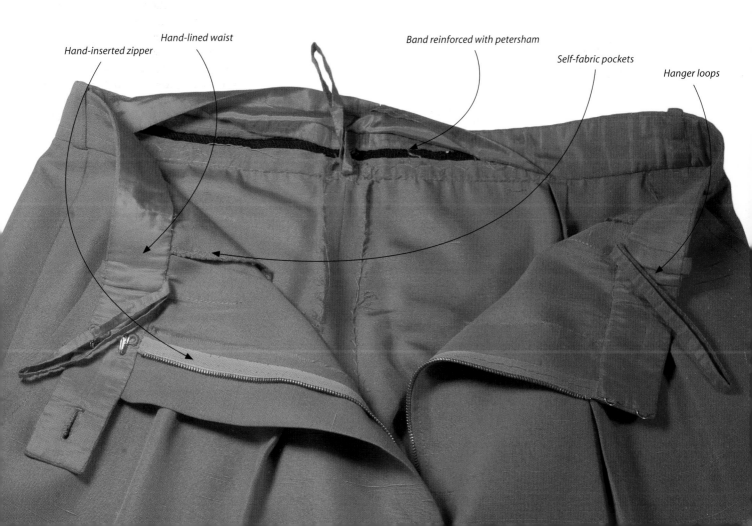

Hand-inserted zipper

Hand-lined waist

Band reinforced with petersham

Self-fabric pockets

Hanger loops

MID-LEVEL READY-TO-WEAR

These everyday, workplace-appropriate garments are made with economy in mind. They need to be presentable, even dressy, but they make no pretensions to luxury.

MEN'S GARMENT FROM BROOKS BROTHERS

This first example is a pair of men's linen pants from Brooks Brothers. On the outside, they look more like the YSL pants than the jeans—with their pleats, creases, and unobtrusive side-seam pockets—but on the inside, they're more like the jeans. They're distinguished from the previous pants by the lining and shaping of the fly shield and by the welted, buttoning rear pockets, whose bags extend up to and are caught in the waistband seam. All are examples of bulk reduction compared to the jeans in these areas.

All the narrow pocket and garment side seam allowances are caught together with serging and are pressed to the back. You can just make out the seams of a tiny patch pocket inside the left-front pocket bag. The waistband is a simple strip, not stiffened or reinforced. There may be some light fusible interfacing inside, but it's not obvious, so this waist is softer than either the jeans or the YSL bands. As on the YSL pants, the waistband is lined rather than self-faced.

The center-back seam appears to be the only seam whose allowances are pressed open. All the rest are pressed to one side. Note that, like both our bookend garments by L.L. Bean and YSL, the waistband is not broken at the center back.

This Brooks Brothers garment is an example of modern workplace ready-to-wear with classic details and minimal structure.

The soft-lined band catches the pocket bags. The front bags are finished with the side seams.

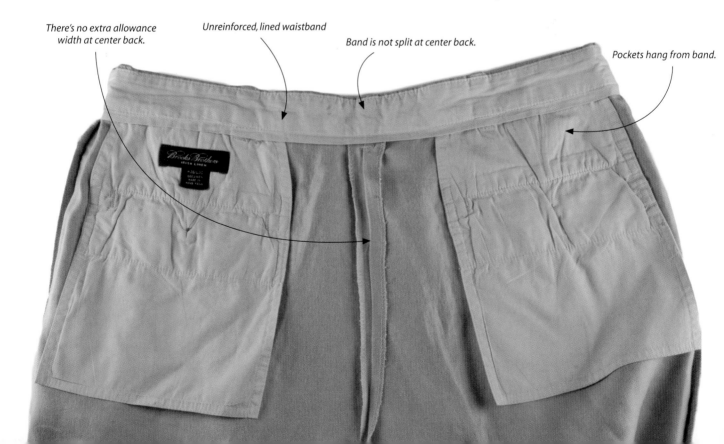

There's no extra allowance width at center back.

Unreinforced, lined waistband

Band is not split at center back.

Pockets hang from band.

All the pockets extend to the band stitching. The front pockets do not extend to the side seams.

WOMEN'S PANTS BY MARY ELLEN FLURY

This women's garment is a pair of woolen pants made by designer and sewing teacher Mary Ellen Flury, based on her years of experience in factory ready-to-wear production. A notable new feature is the absence of a separate waistband structure. The fronts and back have simply been extended upward and shaped above the side seams and darts to create the band, eliminating a waistband/garment seam.

The front pockets are neatly welted into the front piece, not formed as part of the side seam. The bags inside don't extend to and aren't caught in the side seams, although they are extended upward so as to be caught in the topstitching that secures the lower edge of the self-fabric waist facing.

The band area is about as soft and unstiffened as the Brooks Brothers pants. Note that the fly shield is not lined, but simply folded over at the front and seamed at top and bottom. It meets the band on the left inside in a surprisingly thick lump. The bag of the single-welted back pocket has a similar treatment.

In the back, we encounter our first split waistband, separated above the center-back seam. The allowances widen substantially from bottom to top, allowing for future alteration here if needed.

Side and inseam allowances are pressed open, and there's a dramatic belt loop above the front pleats, widened to match the spacing between the pleats.

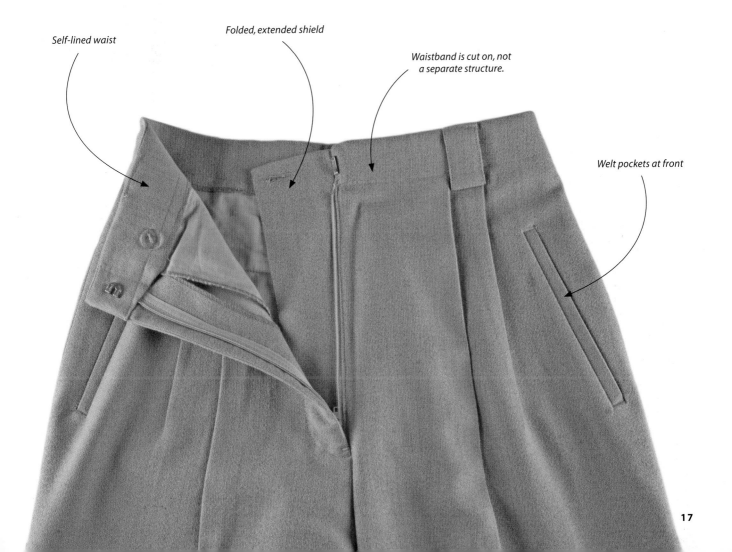

Self-lined waist

Folded, extended shield

Waistband is cut on, not a separate structure.

Welt pockets at front

ORVIS CHINOS

Despite its unassuming exterior, this second men's example introduces more features: the most complex waistband we've yet seen, plus an extended fly-shield lining and a front crotch reinforcement or stay. These cotton twill chinos, or khakis, from Orvis have narrow side seam allowances that are pressed open (although they've come unpressed from laundering).

The waistband is elaborate. It's pieced, with a little green piping inserted between the top and bottom pieces. It's also multilayered, concealing three different types of interfacing or stiffening. This is the first band we've seen whose lining or facing doesn't extend all the way to the front on the overlap side. The outer band is folded around the fly front so the band-lining layers don't start until after the fly. From this and other details, it's clear that bulk reduction was NOT on the mind of the designer of these pants.

The rear seams of the front pocket bags are folded over the side seams and secured to just the rear side of the seam allowance, not serged all together. Note the widened seam allowances at center back.

The fly shield is shaped to include a buttonhole below the waistband. Its lining extends considerably at the bottom, going well beyond the shield itself. This extension has been formed into a narrow, tubular reinforcement for the front crotch seam and is stitched to the seam allowances there to about 2 inches (5.1 cm) beyond the inseam.

Tucked into the inseam and front crotch seam stitching on each side are small triangular pieces of pocketing, which act as reinforcements called crotch or fork stays.

The entire waistband is split to be expandable at the sides and also the back, with the aid of a clever split at the front edges of the front pocket bags. The bands in front attach only to the pants side of the pocket bag, covering the side band layers, which attach only to the body side of the pocket bag, thus doubling the already very thick band just over the front pockets. All this deserves a closer look, which we'll give in a later section on expanding pockets.

The lined, shaped shield has a buttonhole and extends into the crotch seam. Notice the split-top pockets.

These Orvis chinos have plain fronts that conceal a complex, expanding waistband.

The multilayer band lining is split at back. Green piping is inserted between the top and bottom layers.

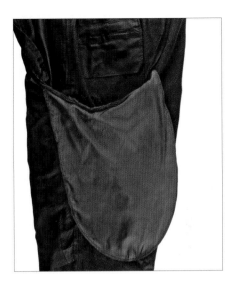

Thigh shields are attached only at the crotch seam.

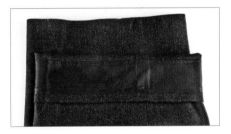

The hem edge is machine-stitched to the lining, which is hand-stitched to the garment.

HIGH-LEVEL READY-TO-WEAR

Unlike the previous garments, the next two have definite pretensions to luxury, in keeping with their cost and their august branding. Armani is a world-renowned designer, of course. Oxxford is a venerable, top-drawer U.S. tailoring house.

WOMEN'S GARMENT BY GIORGIO ARMANI

Giorgio Armani created this women's garment in wool flannel, an excellent example of his signature adaptation of menswear styling for women's wear. Bulk reduction is again a feature of this waistband, with a single layer of petersham forming the lightly fused band's lining. Petersham is a good choice because both its edges are selvages, so it can simply be edge-stitched to the outer band's top seam allowance to complete the band edge.

This waistband is split at center back (with plenty of seat seam allowance for alteration), and it extends into a tab beyond the center front overlap like the YSL garment; but here, the tab portion is faced with outer fabric, not lined to the end.

All four pockets are made of lining fabric, not pocketing cotton or self-fabric, which has been the norm in the garments already examined. The front bags hang free of the side seams, as on the Flury example on page 17. We're also seeing our first garment lining here: a quarter-lining that extends only to the knee level in front and is serged into the side seams, which have narrow, pressed-open seam allowances.

What are these odd, flaplike things falling from the middle of the crotch seam? There's one on each side, so I can only imagine them to be thigh shields because that's the body area they cover. Each one is a double layer of lining serged all around and caught in the crotch seam.

Bulk is reduced at the hem, despite the lightness of the fabric, with the addition of a lining strip covering the raw hem edge; this strip gets secured to the garment.

This Armani garment for women has double-welt pockets in front. The belt loops are caught in the band seam.

The waist is lined with petersham. The pockets are cut from lining fabric.

MEN'S PANTS FROM OXXFORD

These men's trousers are a splendid cuffed garment in wool whipcord (with a different-colored wrong side) from Oxxford Clothes. The main innovation here is inside, where the pocket bags in front and back have been extended, and in back have been shaped all the way to the top of the bands to serve both as waist linings and pockets. The pocket-mouth and fly topstitching are hand-worked with tiny backstitches that catch only a few outer threads with each pass.

Note the split waist treatment: In front is a conventional band, but it ends at the side seam, where the band becomes an extension of the backs. This front band is the first we've seen in which the band/garment seam allowances have been pressed open for a smooth, flat finish. All the other garments with bands have had their waist seam allowances pressed up and enclosed inside the band.

The seam allowances are extended at center back and at the rear side seam. The extra-wide side seam might be both an adjustment allowance and a bit of added weight for the seam, as in the YSL pants on page 15.

In front, extra strips of folded-up pocketing have been inserted between the pockets and the fly to cover the band, which has been stiffened all around with a crisp synthetic canvas. This pocket-becomes-band-lining scheme is wonderfully clever, efficient, and bulk free; but it requires hand stitching along the entire upper edge and at each vertical join between pocket bags.

In front is the expected shield lining, here extended a bit below the fly opening à la Orvis (page 18). Also, the lining attaches to a floating crotch shield reminiscent of the Armani thigh flaps (page 19), in that these are doubled lining layers attached only to the crotch seam, with edges free on each side.

A buttonhole tab extends from the shield up to a button at the waist. A little patch pocket is placed inside the right-front pocket bag.

The fly opening is slightly curved at the bottom and cut and formed so it extends below the straight portion of the center front seams—the first such fly opening we've seen so far in this tour.

These men's trousers from Oxxford have a split-band finish at the waist. The front band ends at the side seams.

The waistband and garment seam is pressed open. Notice the tab inserted into the shield edge.

The pocket bags extend to form the band lining. There's an extra-wide seam allowance at center back.

The fly shield extends into the crotch seam. The lining is attached to a floating crotch shield.

MEN'S AND WOMEN'S CUSTOM-TAILORED TROUSERS

I've included two examples of custom work from my friend and mentor, Seattle tailor and teacher Stanley Hostek, who lent me garments he made for himself and his wife. They're basic dress garments, with no frills or extras that might be added to custom garments intended for a client.

The men's pair, shown here, offers us another clear example of a deep, curved-zipper fly opening. Stanley's wife's pants, shown on page 23, share many features with his, but are more conventionally handled inside. The band is similarly pressed smooth where it meets the trousers, but the zipper isn't curved, and the belt loops are caught in the waist/garment seam.

MEN'S GARMENT BY STANLEY HOSTEK

The edges of the pocket mouths are simple folds, not bulky seams. The waistband/garment seam has its allowances beautifully pressed open. The waistband is not uniformly wide, but tapers down a bit toward the back, and is not joined above the center back seam.

Note the hand-overcast edge finish on all seam allowances and the extra allowance width at center back and sides.

The belt loops aren't caught in waistband seams, either at top or bottom. Instead, they're stitched to the surface of the garment or the band.

Inside, there's clearly a common ancestry with the Oxxford pair on the facing page, with the similar treatment where pockets meet waist. It's a little more obvious in the Hostek garment how the rear seams of the front pockets are secured to the side seam allowances.

On these pants by Stanley Hostek, the band and garment seam is pressed open.

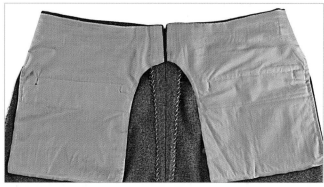

The pocket bags finish the band. The center-back seam allowances are overcast-stitched by hand. The split band at center back allows for ease of movement.

The belt loops are not caught in the band seam. The button tab on the back pocket is formed from a tube, just like the loops.

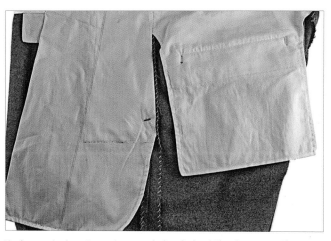

The front pocket bags, inserted at an angle, line the band. There's an extra-wide rear side-seam allowance.

Scraps of pocketing are inserted between the pockets and the fly at the band.

Heel stays are inserted by hand at the back crease.

A watch pocket is inserted in the top edge of the waist lining.

The shield tab is made from pocketing fabric. The shield extends over the crotch seams.

A small square of lining is added at the knee to reduce bagging.

In front, note how carefully the allowances of the waistband/fly seams above the zipper are pressed open, requiring intricate integration between the fly-making steps and the waistband-making steps.

The fly-shield lining is neatly extended into a crotch-seam reinforcement as in the Orvis chinos (page 18), and a pair of crotch stays has been inserted into the inseams.

At the knee, there's a small square of lining caught in the side and inseams, intended to reduce bagging. At the hem, little strips of self fabric are inserted over the hem allowance in back as heel stays.

It might take one a while to notice that there's a little watch or ticket pocket inserted into the lining at the waistband's upper edge. The Oxxford trousers (page 20) had one of these, too.

WOMEN'S GARMENT BY STANLEY HOSTEK

Like the men's garment, this pair has a buttonhole tab extended from the shield. Inside, the shield lining reinforces the crotch, along with stays. The side and center-back seam allowances are extra wide as on the men's garment, and the pocket bag in front tacks into the side seams.

The waist finish is completely different from the men's garment. To accommodate for the expansion from the waist circumference to the hip circumference, it's a two-part arrangement—split between the single-layer lining above and a folded curtainlike portion below that has clearly been given more fullness or extra length than the lining. The curtain allows the waist lining to fit smoothly directly behind the band and to match its width.

Below the lining, the pressed-open allowances and the edge of the canvas waist reinforcement can extend over the garment without being seen. The canvas's lower edge has been clipped about ¼ inch (6 mm) deep at intervals all along, to allow it to expand along with the curtain.

The band of Hostek's women's garment is finished with a "curtain" below the band lining. The canvas interfacing, clipped at intervals, is covered by the curtain.

The band and garment seam is pressed open. A shield tab was added. The shield extends over the crotch seam, and the fork is stayed with the lining.

Band

Center-back seam outlets

Curtain

Pocket edge is stitched to side seam.

MEN'S VINTAGE CUSTOM-TAILORED TROUSERS

The following garments, discards from a first-rate costume collection that had no room for menswear, are now the glories of my tiny collection. They're fine examples of money-was-no-object vintage craftsmanship at the highest level. I wish you could feel the exceptional fabrics and see the workmanship up close!

NEW YORK CITY, 1932

A hand-lettered label hidden inside these magnificent tweed trousers indicates that they were made in New York City in 1932. This garment is a wonderful example of very high-quality, hand-tailored workmanship and materials. It exemplifies the heritage of many of the construction features we've noted in the other samples in this tour so far.

Notice how the back bands taper slightly as did Stanley's (page 21) and how the back itself is angled upward dramatically in relation to the front—rather than continuing more or less straight across and parallel to the front, as do the backs on more modern, belt-supported trousers.

The raised back band in this vintage pair of trousers is a typical feature of trousers supported by suspenders. The side-seam adjustment tabs can take over when suspenders aren't worn.

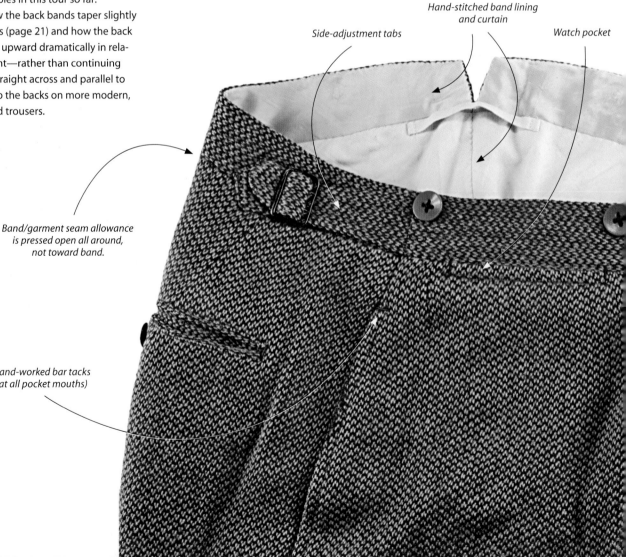

Hand-stitched band lining and curtain

Side-adjustment tabs

Watch pocket

Band/garment seam allowance is pressed open all around, not toward band.

Hand-worked bar tacks (at all pocket mouths)

Starting at the waist, there are minimally interfaced and completely unstiffened bands, with suspender buttons and side-seam adjustment tabs, that are unjoined at the center-back to provide spring. ("Spring" is Stanley Hostek's term for the extra room for movement this provides above the waist.)

Side-seam adjustment tabs, which are typical of the era on trousers without belt loops, allow them to be snugged in when suspenders aren't being worn. These are cut-on extensions to the front band fabric, so it's clear that each main trouser piece, the two fronts and two backs, has a separate waistband finish. There's a watch pocket on the waistband seam.

The band/garment seam allowances have all been pressed open. The bands themselves are beautifully lined with thin silk, hand-stitched to the outer band fabric above and joined to an extensive pleated cotton curtain below.

The button-fly closure is longer at both the top and the bottom, compared to modern pants, reflecting both the high waistline position fashionable at the time (at the natural waist a few inches [centimeters] above the navel) and the extension of the fly opening so far toward the inseam.

The extended buttonhole tab has been cut onto the self-fabric button strip inside the fly, not seamed on. This strip became the fly shield when zippers became the norm.

Note the piecing between the fly buttons, shown in the bottom left photo on page 26, interesting proof that carefully managed and unobtrusive economies of fabric aren't out of place in an obviously luxurious garment.

The fly shield is a button strip on a button fly (1). Notice the fork stays (crotch reinforcements) (2) and the shield's extension into the crotch curve (3).

Split bands at center back provide "spring."

All the seam allowances in this entire fly structure have been painstakingly pressed open, allowing an in-seam buttonhole to be formed for the lower of the two center-front waist buttons. All buttonholes are, of course, hand-worked, as are the bar tacks at each pocket.

Note the clever treatment of the cuff hem. The hem is inserted between the cuff and the pants leg, instead of being folded directly inside the legs. Unlike a folded hem, the inserted hem won't catch on toes when the wearer is slipping on the pants.

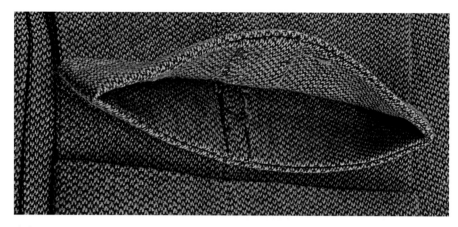

The hem is inserted between the cuff and the pants leg.

The tab extension is cut onto the button strip. Notice the length of the fly.

The band lining is finished by hand. Notice the in-seam placement of the bottom buttonhole.

The knee lining has hand-picked and pinked edges. Notice the extra-wide rear seam allowance.

These classic Italian-made trousers have a button-strip tab and an on-seam waist button. The soft band is hand-lined.

There's hand-stitched topstitching on the fly. The fly opening curves between the legs.

The pocket facings are cut smaller on the selvage to reduce bulk.

The curtain, which covers the band/garment seam, is inserted only in back. In front, it's replaced by pocket bags.

MILAN, ITALY, 1973

This last garment is also magnificent, in a less obviously vintage way. Made in Milan and dated 1973, these trousers are distinguished by their fabric: an extraordinarily smooth and fine twill. The garment is unusual, also, in the absence of either belt loops or suspender buttons.

All seam allowances around the completely unstiffened band are pressed open, and everything is so flat that even the watch pocket behind the pleat folds would be barely detectable, were it not for the little hand-worked bar tacks scattered so liberally about. The button strip's lining extends to the inseam, and the lining of the fly overlap wraps around the buttonhole strip behind it as a hand-felled binding. Even the hidden watch pocket's bag has been turned and stitched. A masterpiece, from start to finish.

The pocket mouths and fly are almost imperceptibly hand-picked, and the back-pocket welts seem almost painted on, so smoothly do they lie against the backs, with no visible topstitching or tacking—proof that the welt seam allowances, too, have been pressed open, as I'll describe on page 67. Note how similarly the button fly is treated compared to the New York City example— from the shape of the cut-on buttonhole extension to the inseam buttonhole above it—and how nicely the fly opening, extended well into the crotch curve, tucks between the draping legs.

Inside the front pockets, the facings have been cut on the selvages to allow them to be secured without folding under a raw edge, for maximum flatness.

Below the pockets, the side seam allowances are pressed, without clipping, toward the front, creating a distinctive rear-facing ridge or welt that's also been delicately hand picked from top to bottom. The quarter-lining is cut on the cross grain so the lining selvage can form a bulkless hem just below the knee.

Inside, the waistband is lined with hand-stitched silk and stitched to a deep curtain that extends over the pockets only in back.

A FEW CONCLUSIONS

So, which are the best techniques for constructing pants from the diverse (but hardly comprehensive) collection of pants-making options presented in this tour? I'll share my conclusions here, but feel free to differ and to draw your own, too. First, some general observations.

• It's the fabric, not the features

Despite my regard for painstaking, even spectacular, workmanship, it's far more critical to my enjoyment of a pair of pants that the fabrics, inner and outer, feel good and wear well. This aspect is more critical than whether, say, the band is cut on or added, or whether the fly shield is extended at the bottom or not. In short, the impact of these different finishing techniques and construction details on wearing comfort will almost always be quite subtle.

• Works for her, works for him

Try as I might, I cannot find a single technique, finish, or detail in these four garments that I'd consider only appropriate for a woman's garment OR for a man's garment (except for the lack of a fly shield on the YSL pants, page 15). When making pants for myself, as long as I'm happy with the style on the outside, I feel completely free to use any construction detail I like on the inside. Prime example: splitting the band at center back or not—neither choice is gender specific. Choose whichever treatment you'd like. If you're interested in adding some "gender" to your project, do it with color and fabric.

• Practicality rules

For me, any choice about which technique or finishing effect to use ultimately comes down to two issues: Do I like the look AND do I think it's worth my time to reproduce it? For example, although I greatly admire hand-stitched bar tacks and pick-stitched outlining, I'm not willing to spend the time to perfect and then apply those techniques. So, I'm quite content with machine topstitching and am interested in finding ways to make that look great. I have one notable exception, however: There's no easy way to machine-stitch the pocket tops to the top edge of the band or pants when creating a band facing à la Oxxford (page 20) or Hostek (pages 21–23), so I'm perfectly willing to hand-finish them—on the inside of the garment—in my amateurish way.

Construction Details and Preferences

Here's a point-by-point run-down on what I saw and liked in the garments on the tour. I'll also specify the options I'd like to include in my own pants. These construction details are the focus of the remaining chapters of the book—and the basis of the variations explored on the companion DVD. For me, making pants is all about the fabric and those specific details I can see or feel in the finished garment.

WAISTBANDS

Cut-on waistbands—I prefer cut-on bands to sew-on bands any day. A cut-on band is less work, and I think it looks more elegant, too. When I do make a pair of pants with an add-on band, however, I'm sure to press open the band/garment seam allowances as much as possible to keep everything flat and smooth. I also split the band at the center back to allow for easy alteration.

Are cut-on bands less comfortable because you can't ease the pants onto a separate band? Not in my experience, but others may disagree. The pattern changes that create a cut-on band don't change the pants below the waist in any way. The fit (ease) in the pattern remains the same. Do I need "spring" in my britches, created by leaving the top of the center-back seam line open a bit? Not that I've particularly noticed, but why not?

Waistband finishes—Thinner, softer, simpler are better. No curtains for me, if I can help it! Extending the pocket bags to serve as a partial waist finish is a brilliant idea, at least in front. So is using petersham, whenever a band lining is more appropriate. The ribbon can even double as a hook-and-eye stabilizer. Why not combine the two? That's my current practice. I've lost interest in no-roll band stiffeners and can definitely feel the difference. A lightweight fusible, or a linen or other nonstretch woven layer, seems like plenty of body to me, if any is needed at all.

One advantage that a stiff insert provides is a firm, straight edge over which to fold the seam allowances at the top. It's useful, but not essential. Light interfacing helps, too. A waist stiffener gives you something durable on which to attach your hooks and eyes, but it does not need to extend around your entire waist.

Complex waistband and fly constructions—You've seen these elaborate effects, with all seams pressed open, on many of the pants in the tour (especially the custom-made garments). They're great looking but add lots of fiddly effort. I prefer to keep my options open by choosing simple and interchangeable fly and waistband finishes, but you have my blessing to choose otherwise! (Stanley Hostek's book, listed on page 134, covers this type of construction in detail.)

POCKETS

Almost any kind of pocket can look good on tailored pants, possibly even patch pockets. Pockets present a wonderful opportunity for experimenting with new design ideas and variations on old themes. For welt pockets, I like the flat look that comes from pressing open the welt/pant seam allowances. For on-seam pockets, I prefer the pocket-mouth edge to be a folded rather than a seamed edge at the opening, as described in a later chapter.

In back, I generally go for flaps or button tabs rather than buttonholes. They're easier and safer to make because you don't attach them until you've made a good one.

I recommend extending your pocket bags to reach whatever waist finish you've chosen. This way, you can support the bag from the waist rather than only from the pocket mouth.

Are watch/ticket pockets worth the effort? You decide, but notice how much easier it is to place them at the top of the band, as

Stanley Hostek did (page 22), rather than in the band/garment seam line: No facing is needed, and there's no need to open the waist/band seam, if there is one.

CLOSURES

Length of zipper fly—I do like, and can easily duplicate, the look of the button flies on vintage garments as they dip deep between the legs. I also admire Stanley's curved and deep-dipping zipper fly. A subtle effect, to be sure, and not easy to duplicate with a zipper. There are some reasons not to even try: Curved zipper tapes and curved fly seams in general add a lot of complexity to the already treacherous enough fly-making process. You also can't use cut-on facings or shields, which are thinner and softer than the sewn-on ones. If you must have curved zippers, refer to Stanley's book (page 134). But first, check the crotch curve on your chosen pattern; there may not be enough curve there to build your fly on.

Button flies—I prefer a button fly, because zippers often create an imprint on the front, especially in combination with a fly-facing seam. There's also always a lump at the top where the pull sits. Buttons can go as far into the crotch curve as you like. Mostly, it's my fascination with vintage details that makes button flies appeal to me so much.

Fly shields—I would always use a shield. Folding, rather than lining, the shield makes good sense to me, but lined shields are preferable if your shield is cut-on rather than seamed-on, or if you want to shape the outer edge. Extending the bottom of the shield lining to cover and reinforce the crotch seam is a nice touch, but only worth doing if you like the look. I've never had a pair of pants split because of an unreinforced crotch seam, and there's no difference in how the pants feel with or without the extension.

Hooks and eyes—This type of closure is very practical in use, even if something of a pain to install. Buttons and buttonholes are just as practical and tedious, but there's no rethink-

ing a done buttonhole. Hooks and eyes with prongs that poke through the fabric into a metal backing are more secure than sew-in styles, although they're harder to find. They also need a solid interior fabric to hook into. Still, they're my first choice for closures.

Fly buttonhole tabs—You definitely add an extra, if simple, step to extend a shield to include a fly buttonhole tab or to add one in a different fabric. They are kind of fun to use, if you like doing up superfluous closures (I'll admit to that). I can't discern any advantage or feel any difference between having one and not. Check out my Afterthought Pleat Stay on page 121—now that DOES feel different and actually accomplishes something: the stabilizing of your pleats.

INTERIOR FINISHES

Linings (full, quarter, or patch)—I'm personally not a fan of linings in pants, no matter what size. I find them too much trouble to make and those I've had have always made the pants too hot to wear. I don't think any lining fabric ever made could really keep MY knees from bagging out the pants legs. I buy pant fabrics I want to have next to my skin, don't you? If I did like linings, I'd make a few pairs of separate pant liners—sliplike pants in lining fabric that aren't sewn in—so they were entirely optional and washable.

Crotch reinforcements—These reinforcements, otherwise known as fork stays, are in my experience imperceptible in their effect, although they are simple, quick details to add. So why not? As for crotch and thigh shields—Why?

Heel stays—I feel the same way about heel stays as about crotch reinforcements, except heel stays are nowhere near as simple and quick to add, so I skip them.

CHAPTER TWO
TOOLS AND MATERIALS

Having tools and fabrics that don't merely work but are a delight to use is my favorite aspect of the sewing process—actually more than having the finished products, truth be told! In this chapter, I'll present all my preferences and prejudices regarding notions and fabrics for your consideration. There are no hard-and-fast rules here. This is just an overview of my experiences and opinions, so feel free to ignore these suggestions if your experiences and opinions are different.

SEWING AND PRESSING TOOLS

There are no special, necessary tools for making pants with the techniques in this book—other than those that any sewer would normally have in the sewing-room tool kit—but here are a few items that I've found are nice to have on hand. See Sources on page 132 and the companion DVD for information on where to find specific items.

CLIPPING SCISSORS
My favorite clippers are Gingher's Knife-Edge Tailor's Point Scissors, shown above, but anything similar—strong scissors 4 or 5 inches (10 or 13 cm) short, with razor-sharp blades that clip right to their points, through many layers, every time, such as J. A. Henckels, Kai, or Dovo embroidery scissors—will do splendidly.

THIMBLE
Essential to basting, and indeed to any hand-stitching, is a comfortable thimble. I like my traditional tailor's version, shown above, with its open end—ventilated!

TAILOR'S BASTING THREAD
I hated the very idea of basting until I saw Stanley Hostek at work (EVERY step is basted first) and tried the special thread he uses for it: a glazed, white cotton that doesn't kink, shred, or catch, and slips out easily. You can stitch right over it, unlike pins, and you can try on basted garments without danger—what a revelation!

This traditional trade material, called No. 40 basting thread (white; 2 oz. [57 g]), shown below, changed everything for me in the basting vs. pinning debate. A 750-yard (686 m) spool costs about $5 and will last you a long time, unless you're tailoring all day, every day. You'll see it in use in the video tutorials on the companion DVD.

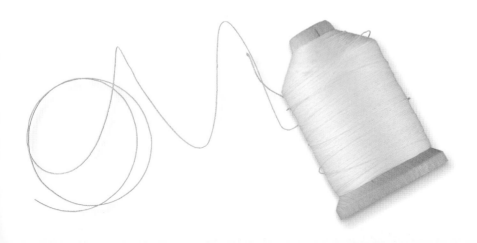

HEMOSTATS

These fabulously useful, gripper/point-turners are my latest discovery. I love them! Actually, I've had a pair around for a long time, bought and sometimes used as a needle puller, which is one of the intended purposes for this common surgeon's tool. I only recently learned about their additional role as great point-turners, thanks to Pam Erny, from the Creative Machine mailing list. In addition to offering a firm grip and smooth, strong, and tiny tips, they've got a simple locking function, so you can squeeze them shut, hook the handles together, and let go without losing your grip. You'll see them in use in photos later in the book and in the videos on the companion DVD.

AWL

I like to have a sturdy awl nearby. It's useful for controlling fabric layers as they travel under the presser foot and handy whenever you need a sturdy pointed thing.

WOODEN PRESSING SURFACES

Padded surfaces are only part of the pressing story. For a really sharp crease or edge, you need to press against a wooden surface. My assorted favorites are shown in the photo below, including a clever Seam Stick from Belva Barrick. This half-dowel wooden object is perfect for opening long leg seams in one go. Even if you make only one pair of pants a year, you'll love having it.

A tailor board (the complex-curved item in the photo) is great for opening short and curved seams. This wonderful tool is unfortunately no longer being made by the June Tailor company, but you might be able to find one on ebay.com or at an estate sale.

There are several sources for similar pressing tools listed in Sources on page 132, but you could also settle quite happily for a more basic straight-edged point presser. You can usually use the base of such a presser as a clapper, too, at least in the clapper's usual role, which is to apply pressure to something you've just pressed without adding any further heat from the iron. Because I actually use mine most frequently as a flat, wooden, pressing surface for stuff that's too big for an edge-pressing tool, I particularly like the large clapper I got from Cecelia Podolak. The flat surfaces of the tailor board and its clones work well for this purpose, too, as does a cheese block, also available from Cecelia.

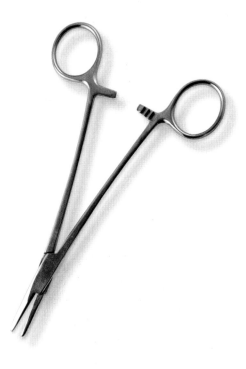

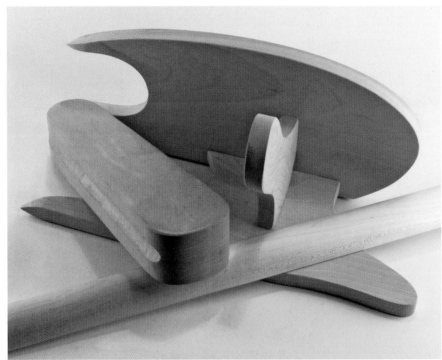

THE DRY IRON

My dry-iron enthusiasm derives from a personal pet peeve: I hate an iron that leaves imprints from its steam holes when pressing on my gorgeous fabric, so I use an antique, hole-less iron that glides like butter and lets me perfectly control the steam by forcing me to spray or daub on water only when and where I need it. (It's a Sunbeam Ironmaster, shown above; I have several.) I know I'll never convince you to stop buying (and endlessly replacing) your fancy steamer, but you can still get a dry version online. It's inexpensive, too!

If you're even mildly dissatisfied or uncertain about the results you're getting with an iron, check out Cecelia Podolak's pressing video listed in Sources, page 132. It'll move you out of laundry-room mode and into the tool-master's circle in a hurry.

GLUING SUPPLIES AND MARKING TOOLS

Whenever I mention glue in a sewing workshop or class, everybody laughs, as if I'm cheating or something. Apparently, the word hasn't yet gotten out: Adhesives are a sewer's best friend! They're the tiny fingers you don't have and the invisible pins that don't ever need to come out. Admittedly, I'm quite restrained here. I use only a water-soluble glue stick and, recently, a neat ultra-fine fusible basting tape (see Sources, page 132)—so far, no spray adhesives or glue guns—but, really, you have to try these things! I hope that, as you read through the construction sections of the book, you'll see my point.

Three quick glue-stick tips: Don't use more than you need, which is usually very little. Dry the glued place with an iron when you're using it to hold a little fold or edge in place, so you can easily reopen and re-do the fold if it isn't quite right yet. Don't use the glue if it's dried out and shrunken in the tube. (You can often resuscitate a shriveled glue stick by spraying some water into the tube cover, snapping it on tight, and letting it sit overnight—but this stuff is cheap, so get a new tube now and again.)

To me, gluing supplies and marking tools are in the same category: They're indispensable facilitators of precision results. When it comes to marking, the word is no doubt out about the refillable chalk wheel. It's the essential tool, especially for wool. Add a cheap, medium-stiff brush for erasing the chalk, and you're all set.

As far as I'm concerned, you simply can't have too many transparent rulers. Every new one you see, go ahead and buy it—you need it. Ideally, it will be marked with a $1/8$-inch (3 mm) grid, not just every $5/8$ inch (6.4 mm). I find these finer markings very helpful when straightening raw edges with my rotary cutter.

THREAD

All-polyester, three-ply thread is my default choice for almost all pants-making because it's so strong. I do love sewing with silk threads and definitely use them on the best woolens (except at the crotch seams, where polyester still seems wisest). I avoid wrapped threads completely and reserve my cotton threads for shirts and for buttonholes. Simple rules, and not much scrutinized as they have yet to fail me.

OUTER AND INNER FABRICS

There's an oft-repeated bit of sewing terminology that distinguishes between top- and bottom-weight fabrics. The idea is that some fabrics are too heavy for top garments, such as blouses and shirts, while others are too light for bottom garments, like skirts and pants. Although this may seem true in general (and obviously true in extremes), in my experience such distinctions are well worth questioning. Certainly there are many fabrics that won't make up into traditional-looking and -feeling pants, but the fabrics that will go way beyond the typical, reliable, and conventional pants fabrics, especially once you venture outside of standard uniforms for school, church, and office and into leisure and sportswear.

Transparency, crispness, and wrinkle resistance seem to me to be much more critical factors in any fabric's trouser-worthiness than weight or thickness. I'd absolutely consider many shirt-weight fabrics as suitable for pants, and vice versa. The same distinctions can be made, and equally well challenged, between outer and inner (pants and pocketing) fabrics. I've rarely met a pocketing that I wouldn't also consider for light- to medium-weight pants (not counting the silky lining fabrics often used in women's pants)—and I've got plenty of fabrics that I still haven't sorted (pants, pockets, shirts?). Allow yourself the fun of questioning the rules! Or at the very least, consider that something you might have bought for a shirt could make really nice pants pockets, too.

The grading is often woven into the selvage of wool fabric.

I'm definitely a bit of a natural-fiber-fabrics snob, because I know they'll always take a crease well (definitely a plus—I hate to fight the fabric!) and because they'll most likely breathe and be comfortable to wear. So, I can't speak from experience about all the microfibers and spandex blends that many sewers and manufacturers are using these days, apparently with much success. Never one to ignore a reason to buy some new fabric, I plan on rectifying this omission soon.

Although I've made (and will make) many cotton and linen pants, there's no question in my mind that wool is the preeminently perfect fabric for pants, even in warm weather. Wool sheds wrinkles and tends not to cling, all while pressing beautifully. It's amazing how silken and resilient a very fine woolen can be, and how lightweight. Many people have never seen or touched really good quality woolens, in which these virtues are even more noticeable than in the best shirting cottons, simply because they're so expensive. These fabrics don't show up in ready-to-wear or fabric shops, except at the highest end. To find out for yourself, I recommend checking out any local tailors you may have in your area (the more exclusive, the better), both to see example swatches and to discuss buying yardage—you might just discover a willing mentor (or fitter) in the process.

Like shirting fabrics, wools for tailoring are often graded by number on the basis of thread diameter (the higher numbers indicate higher quality and finer threads). These numbers are often woven right into the selvage, as shown in the photo above. The really deluxe stuff starts at around 120 and goes as high as 200. Most fabric stores that carry fine woolens sell 80s as their high end. You should treat yourself at least once to a for-fondling-only visit to a really expensive clothing store, both to feel the fabrics and to check out the details and finishing. A men's store is somewhat more likely to have woolens of the type I'm describing and is definitely more likely to have beautifully made trousers to examine. Consider this necessary training for yourself as a garment maker; progress in any craft is as much a matter of constantly raising one's standards as it is of refining one's skill.

A caveat: The finer and more smoothly finished the woolen, the less forgiving it is. Medium-weight woolens with soft, flanneled

Wool fabrics are the perfect fabrics for trousers.

surfaces are among the easiest of fabrics to sew because they conceal stitches and can be steam-shaped and both overpressed and unpressed without complaining. Not so the smooth-faced, ultra-thin woolens, which is why testing is critical (see sidebar at right).

I made my all-time favorite pants, now sadly deceased, from a deliciously crisp but soft, wool-cotton blend in a loose but stable, open weave. These were the most comfortable summer pants I've ever worn—wrinkle-resistant, not a scratch in them, and transparent to the slightest puff of breeze but not to light. My eye is constantly peeled for similar yardage. I haven't found it yet, but the original fabric did alert me to the potential of great natural-fiber-and-wool blends. Let me know if you find any!

If you're considering laying out the fronts and backs in different directions to save yardage, by all means stitch up a small test. Then move it around in various lights to see if there's any nap or directional flavor to its woven pattern, texture, or even its sheen. Many traditional trouser fabrics, including most twills and other diagonal textures, are designed to be directionless simply to allow such layout economy—but you don't want to find out otherwise when it's too late! Learn what you need to know BEFORE you cut. Of course, there's no way to test a fabric thoroughly without actually making it into a garment and wearing it around for a while; but, in the long run, every garment you make is a test, right?

TEST YOUR FABRIC FIRST!

No matter what the fabric is made of, if you're attracted to a fabric that seems to have qualities that differ from what you're used to sewing, do yourself a favor and buy at least an extra ¼ yard (23 cm) so you'll feel free to experiment with it a bit, especially if it's expensive, made from a fiber you haven't worked with before, or is softer, more loosely woven, or more slippery than what you typically choose. You'll want to try it with various weights and types of interfacing. Stitch some seams into it at various angles to the straight grain; rip some of these a little, pressing them open and tugging on them sideways, especially if the fabric is loosely woven or soft; make some creases and do some topstitching; test thread colors—and maybe even make a test pocket or fly front.

POCKETING FABRICS

With the help of great fabrics, pockets are easy to do in high style. I use only garment-quality all-cotton twills or sateens for my front pants pockets. The stuff sold for pocketing at tailoring suppliers is NOT garment quality; it's an interior fabric that you'd never choose as a garment fabric. I use only the smoothest, glossiest, and most silk-like fabrics I can find. In fact, I collect choice pocketing prospects and have a happy struggle with every new project over which jewel to bring into the mix. What better place to use an over-$25-per-yard fabric than for an application needing only a half-yard (46 cm)

Choose the most silk-like pocketing fabrics you can find.

that you'll enjoy touching dozens of times on every wearing?

Notice I said front pockets? I see no reason to overburden rarely used rear pockets (well, I rarely use them) with the same sturdy pocketing that I usually want in front, especially if my garment fabric is medium weight or heavier, so I've often opted for a lining-type or lining-weight fabric in back. Why use the same fabric for all pockets? Only if you or the intended pants-wearer thinks it's important to do so. I like shirting scraps for my thinner pocket bags.

Shiny, slick, lining fabrics—in rayon, poly, silk, or acetate—are, of course, frequently found in RTW women's pants pockets, as are self-fabrics (the garment's outer fabric in hidden or interior uses, such as pockets and interfacings), but I've never chosen them for front pockets. If you enjoy slipping your hands into a pocket made of one of these fabrics, go for it. (Flannel-sheet pockets or 500-threads-per-inch, satin-sheet pockets, anyone?) If you'll be putting keys, coins, and other such things in your pockets, consider how your pocketing fabric will hold up to, buffer your legs from, and contain whatever you're likely to store within your pockets. And, of course, make sure your pockets are as preshrunk and/or washable as the rest of your garment.

INTERFACINGS

I use fusible interfacing in four different ways. Fortunately, there are at least four currently available fusible interfacings that serve these various needs perfectly. I've tried and liked the Perfect Fuse offerings from Palmer/Pletsch, but there are definitely others.

Purpose 1: When I need straight-grain stability in some area where my outer fabric is more or less on bias—typically at a pocket mouth. Whether it's an on-seam pocket opening or a welt opening in the middle of a piece, I'll usually add a rectangle of thin woven, knit, or weft-insertion interfacing centered over the opening, with the stable direction of the interfacing parallel to the pocket mouth. These days, interfacings are

Depending on the effect and placement, you can choose from a variety of materials to reinforce waistbands.

available that don't noticeably stiffen the garment fabric, and any of them would be a good choice for this purpose if they have a stable direction. **Type of interfacing:** Perfect Fuse Light by Palmer/Pletsch is a thin, weft-insertion interfacing that creates no stiffening, needs no preshrinking, and offers great stability in one direction.

Purpose 2: When I want to increase the stiffness of a section of the fabric just enough to fold a precise shape over the stiffened part, such as along the edge of a band or inside a shaped belt loop. A piece of old-school, woven fusible is usually just right after it's cut into exactly the finished shape of the needed detail. **Type of interfacing:** Form-Flex by HTCW is a woven fusible that works well, but anything that creates a distinct change in stiffness that you can fold against and is easy to cut into an accurate shape is fine.

Stiffness is what most folks have hated about most fusibles since forever, but there are now plenty of improved choices. I'd choose a woven one for ease of cutting to a precise shape with no curling edges and the like.

Purpose 3: When I want to fasten down any allowances I've folded into a precise shape. I can think of nothing better than a tiny sliver of ultra-thin fusible overlapping the fabric and securing it to the shaping interfacing inside. **Type of interfacing:** Perfect Fuse Sheer by Palmer/Pletsch is an ultra-light weft insertion that won't add to the bulk of a fused shape. Any ultra-thin fusible should do the trick here as so little is needed.

Purpose 4: When I want to increase the density and/or body of a too-thin or too-transparent fabric. Fusing interfacing to entire pattern pieces will add loft to a fabric that is too thin for tailoring. **Type of interfacing:**

Perfect Fuse Tailor ULTRA by Palmer/Pletsch is weft interfacing with a brushed surface that's designed to be fused to entire pattern pieces. It needs preshrinking, but that's easily done by soaking it in warm water and drying over a shower-curtain rod.

WORKING WITH FUSIBLES

Working with fusibles? Not a problem if the garment isn't going into the washer and dryer. If it is, the heat and moisture will activate or reactivate the fusible glue and can cause failures in the adhesion. If you want to apply fusible interfacing to the wrong side of a fabric—to support pocket stitching, for example—you can always lightly fuse for temporary stability, then pull up the edges so they're actually no longer fused. On wools and other dry-cleaned fabrics, fusibles are fine, and I use them as directed without reservation (after testing that they don't show up on the garment face or feel too board-like).

When I make a folded-front zipper fly, as shown on page 80, I sometimes support the fold-over facing/shield areas with a bias-cut, woven fusible, adding a little bias-cut crease softening to an area that's straight-grained. I arrange the stable direction so it is parallel with the curve of the overlap topstitching, generally helping to keep the fly area smooth. The fusible offers the added advantage of automatically securing any raw edges from raveling, so I don't need to overcast the fly facing.

WAISTBAND REINFORCEMENTS

As for waistband reinforcements, I believe less is more—especially after discovering the vintage trousers in the tour, with their soft, unstiffened waists (pages 24–27). I often use a thin, woven fusible strip to create a nice straight edge for folding against, very helpful with band extensions. I also like Stanley Hostek's choice of a single strip of washed, medium-weight linen canvas as a band support. Interesting to note, he recommends cutting the strip slightly off-grain, presumably to provide a little bias flexibility at the lower edge, which is clipped anyway. I'm a bit dubious about whether this would provide any really noticeable effect, but I like the concept.

If you want something with more heft or roll resistance, there are plenty of waistbanding choices to be had from tailoring suppliers—from waistband-stiffening inserts to complete, ready-made waistband finishings (see page 120 and Sources, page 132). As I've mentioned, my current preference is

for milliner's petersham, which acts as finish, reinforcement, and stabilizer all in one, and needs no edge finishing to boot.

To satisfy my occasional inclination to face the waist differently in front and back and to use different pocketings front and back, I've explored using different waist reinforcement strategies for front and back, too—especially when it comes to no-roll solutions. Why add reinforcements in back if the roll problem is only in front? Again, the differences I've observed in my experiments are more visual (the outline or bulk of too much stabilizer on the outside) than tactile (discomfort from either too much or too little reinforcement). My conclusion? Face the pants back with a sturdy cotton or petersham and no reinforcements. Only reinforce the front if it seems necessary, will look better to you, or helps you to fold the band's upper edge in a straight line.

Petersham acts as an all-in-one finish, reinforcement, and stabilizer.

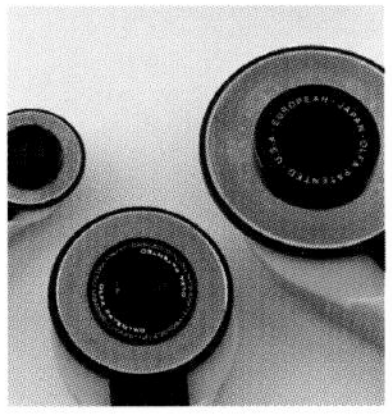

CHAPTER THREE
BASIC CONSTRUCTION

In this chapter and the ones that follow, you'll learn what I choose to do when I make pants. My methods derive from experience, preference, practice, discussions with many experts and fellow sewers over the years, and from lots of close observation (as in Chapter One) and lots of reading. There's a little bit of innovation thrown in here and there, too, but not a lot—thanks to all the mentors and tipsters who have helped add to my skills.

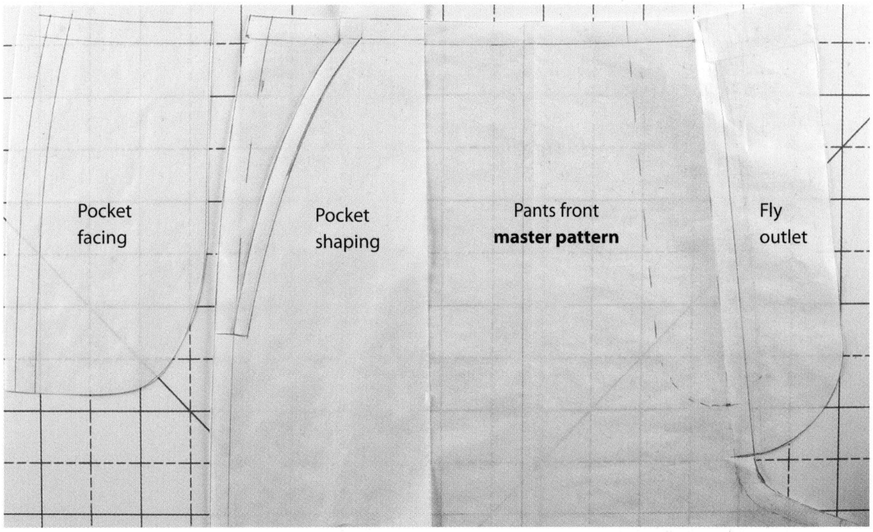

Here's a typical master pattern with a cut-on fly and detail patterns for a specific style of pocket and its facing.

I'd like to be able to say you won't need to look any further than this book and DVD as you perfect your own preferred methods, but that's likely not true. I hope these techniques will give you a useful head start as you learn about making pants, but I also hope (and expect) that you'll keep reading, keep testing, and keep exploring ways to improve your craft. I expect you'll find ways to improve on my methods as you progress toward your ideal pair of pants. I hope you'll let me know when you discover something cool! (You'll find my blog address on the companion DVD.)

MASTER PATTERNS vs. STYLED PATTERNS

I've collected a lot of commercial patterns over the years, but I plunder only details and construction ideas from them. I prefer to approach my projects as variations on a few tried-and-true, fitted patterns with basic but refined silhouettes, whose details may change with each new project, but whose well-known comfort and overall shape I can depend on. It's a "Fit Once, Vary Forever" sort of logic, similar to the process many ready-to-wear and custom-clothing makers use to create new designs from simplified basic patterns they call slopers. The sloper keeps these makers secure in the knowledge that their customers will fit well in their new clothes each time, while enjoying whatever additional features are part of the new look.

So, my pants-pattern collection is actually just one pattern, plus an easily added-to folder full of interchangeable-detail patterns ready to be taped or traced in place as needed. (You'll find some of my favorite detail patterns on the companion DVD, full size, ready to print and use.) It's great not having to fit each new pair of pants I make.

To convert an existing commercial pants pattern into a master pattern or sloper, simply ask yourself what you would need to remove from it to make pants with no details at all: no pockets, no stylized closures or extended waistbands, no belt loops, no yokes, piecings, or extra seams, etc. You should be left with nothing more than one entire front piece, one entire back piece, and some kind of waistband. If you made a muslin test version of your starting styled pattern, you probably eliminated extra details as you made it, so you might simply trace off your muslin and treat that as your master pattern.

Of course, if there are any features that you think you're going to want on future pants, just leave these in place or incorporate them into your master. (For me, it's a cut-on waistband.) Don't hesitate to create a durable, fully styled pattern or two, should you settle on a combination of details that you really like—it'll help you cut out your next identical pair with as little delay as possible.

PANTS CONSTRUCTION

Sometimes, following the right order as you proceed through your pants project is a nonissue (front pockets before back pockets?). At other times, it's obviously critical (attach the waistband after stitching fly and side seams). But it's always crucial to know which time is which, especially if you're working without a pattern guide sheet.

I tend to think of the various pant parts (pockets, fly, waistband, side seams, inseams, and seat seam) as distinct construction units, each one to be basically completed before proceeding to the next, in some preferred order. The simpler your garment and its details are, the more reliable this approach. As details and finishes become more complex, however, construction processes often begin to intersect. Certain steps must

Pants Construction Sequence

1. Darts; then front and back pockets, leaving the front-pocket/side-seam finishing undone
2. Front closure
3. Side seams, front pocket finish
4. Waistband or finish; pleats
5. Inseams
6. Center-back seam
7. Hems

CONSTRUCTING A SIMPLE GARMENT

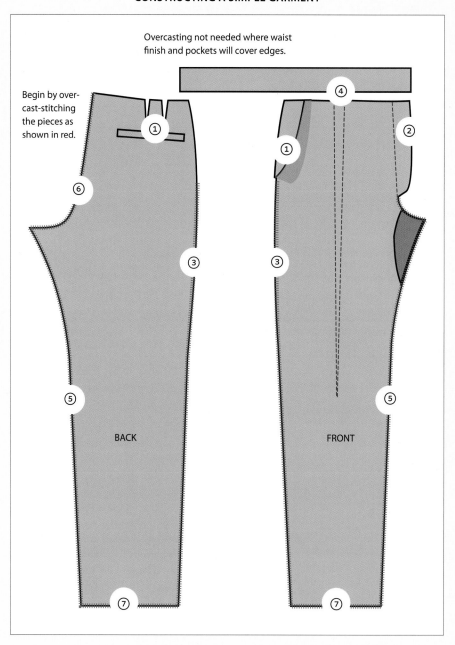

Overcasting not needed where waist finish and pockets will cover edges.

Begin by overcast-stitching the pieces as shown in red.

BACK

FRONT

"The point is to become a fearless and hesitation-free sample maker."

be done in a certain order or sometimes paused, with some stitching left undone, while you bring another process along to a stage that must be completed before you can finish the first process.

As much as I admire the elaborate details that require this complex sequencing, keeping things uncomplicated and flexible is usually a more important consideration for me. Whenever I try out a new detail, change a familiar one, or create a new-to-me combination, I spend a lot of time working through the steps mentally before I cut or sew anything, to make sure I understand how the steps should best go together. In most cases, after I'm pretty sure I have the right sequence in my head, I also make a sample—because it's just not worth it to learn anything at the cost of ruining a project.

A similar logic applies to cutting: Think thrice, cut once! In every way I can, I try to avoid cutting or stitching my way into a corner and try to leave as much of my fabric uncommitted for as long as possible. For example, I usually cut out all of my front pocketing pieces as plain rectangles first. Then, I trim them to match the specific pocket shape I've chosen as I make the pocket.

The point is to become a fearless and hesitation-free sample maker. I keep a stash of sample fabrics nearby, in all my favorite fibers, along with a few bobbins of white and black thread. Armed with an abundance of materials, I can resist letting any fear of waste or delay trump my fear of making a possibly fatal mistake in a finished piece. I've also often whipped out a square or two of fresh paper towel to stitch or staple into a quick, disposable proof of a concept. (I like Viva brand, preferably solid white.) I'll comment on similar sequencing issues and point out other ways to keep options open in all the construction discussions throughout the book.

That said, the first thing I do with my cut-out pant pieces is to overcast-stitch the edges with a wide, long, zigzag stitch, as shown in the drawing on the facing page. Serging or hand-overcasting are good options, too, if you've got the tools or skills. If I've chosen to stay the fork (reinforce the front crotch curve), I'll do that first, so the overcasting catches the stays and holds them in place. The remaining steps usually proceed in the order noted in the box and drawing, unless some styling detail calls for changing it.

ALLOWANCES AND OUTLETS

Whether you're using a styled pattern or a master plus extras, you'll need to consider what size seam allowances to use. You'll also need to consider whether you'll want to include any additional allowances to provide room for future alterations or to create seamless facings. (Tailors call these additions "outlets" or sometimes "inlays").

One of the most striking differences between home-sewing techniques and professional methods is that folks who sew mostly from commercial patterns use the pattern-industry's default seam allowance of $5/8$ inch (1.6 cm) on all pattern edges, while professionals (tailors, dressmakers, factory sewers, sample makers, etc.) almost never use a $5/8$-inch (1.6 cm) seam allowance. These sewers, for whom efficiency is as important as precision, usually prefer a default seam allowance of $1/4$ inch (6.4 mm). They are also very likely to cut out their patterns using different seam allowances on different seams, depending on how they'll be sewing those seams.

So, where did the $5/8$-inch (1.6 cm) seam allowance come from? The short answer is that the home-sewing pattern companies decided long ago that the best way to reduce confusion and complaints about cutting mistakes was to train home sewers always to expect and use the same seam-allowance width everywhere. If a narrower width would make for easier turning or smoother curves, they could simply instruct the customer to trim the allowances. No doubt they settled upon $5/8$ inch (1.6 cm) as a nice, safe width that would provide some wiggle room for inaccurate fitting, stitching, and/or cutting.

Pros don't need the wiggle room. They also have no time to trim down allowances on cut edges, and they can keep track of which seams have which seam-allowance widths if some are different or have outlets. Most important, professional sewers rarely use a cut edge to tell them where the seam line is. In their world, there's often no obvious connection between the shape of the edge and the shape and position of a nearby seam; and, if there's any chance of confusion, they won't hesitate to chalk- or thread-mark the seam line.

Home sewers, in contrast, have generally been trained to assume that the best way to find the seam line is to stitch $5/8$ inch (1.6 cm) inside any cut edge. As a result, they're never likely to have experienced the advantages that can come from having allowances cut at different widths, cut out roughly or in a simplified shape, or cut with outlets of varying widths.

I cut all my pants patterns with $1/4$-inch (6.4 mm) allowances, which pretty much eliminates the need to trim any fabric or clip any curves. I also take full advantage of outlets and rough cutting, as you'll see in the construction photos and videos. I add to my master patterns the outlets that I'll always or usually want—such as extra seam-allowance width at the center back. I include text notes indicating where I need to add outlets while cutting, which makes it easy either to create a custom width or shape or to opt out. When I'm certain, I'll just make physical additions to the pattern outline. If these methods are new to you, give them a try.

SEAM ALLOWANCES AND OUTLETS

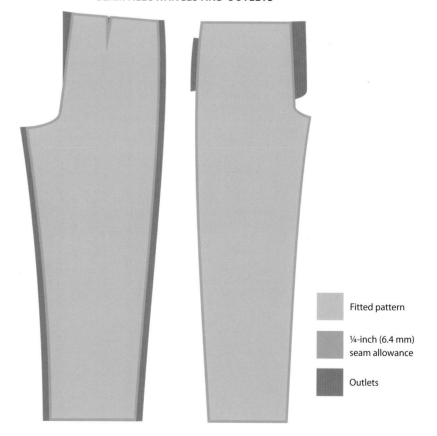

Fitted pattern

¼-inch (6.4 mm) seam allowance

Outlets

BEFORE YOU CUT

Before you begin cutting, decide on any additions you want to make to your pattern, all the specific details you want to incorporate by cutting, and all areas in which you want to leave yourself some options by not cutting quite yet. For example, unless I've decided to use an on-seam pocket and want an outlet, I always cut my fronts without any front pocket shaping—even if I think I'm sure which other pocket I want to use. Later, when I'm ready to make the pockets, it'll be easy to lay out the detail pattern for the pocket opening over the cut-out fronts and trim around it. Waiting gives me yet another chance to reconsider or make final tweaks to the pocket-opening shape, perhaps by drawing up a new detail pattern.

Another way I leave my options open at the cutting stage is never to lay out or cut patterns for the details at the same time that I cut the fronts and backs. I prefer to cut out the details as needed from the scraps, which also encourages me to refold and reexamine the scraps to get the most from them. This approach also lets me double-check each detail's size and shape (for example, pocket-welt lengths) against the main pieces exactly when I need them, as I'm remarking them and thinking about nothing else.

Here are the most likely options you'll need to consider before you start cutting out:

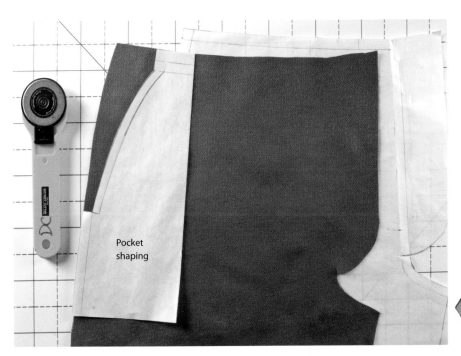

Pocket shaping

The front garment piece is cut out and ready to be styled for pockets.

FRONT POCKETS

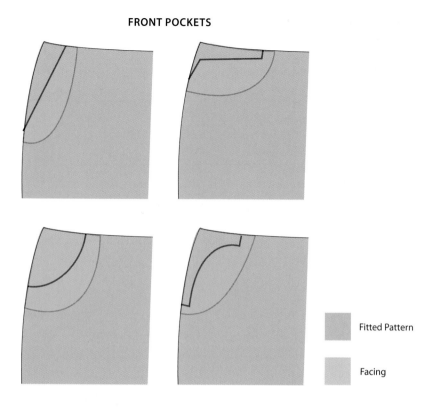

Fitted Pattern

Facing

Front Pockets: If you're choosing any kind of slant-front pockets, you'll need eventually to reshape the front piece to reflect your pocket-opening shape. You'll also need to add a facing piece that restores the side seam and waistline shaping back to the original pant-front outline on its outer edges. As mentioned, however, you may not want to mark or cut out the facing until you're making the pockets. The facing needs to extend beyond the pocket opening on its inner edges, as shown in the drawing at left.

If you're choosing on-seam pockets, decide whether you want to provide a cut-on outlet, as described in the directions on page 51. I would stitch on a facing only if I'd forgotten to cut on an outlet, had decided to go on-seam after cutting out the front, or was piping an on-seam opening—but the difference is slight.

CUT-ON FLY PATTERN

CENTER-BACK AND SIDE SEAMS

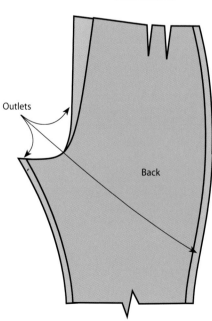

2½"
(6.4 cm)

Pants front

1"

Outlets

Back

Fly: Do you want cut-on zipper facings (outlets), as shown in the drawing at far left, or will you seam these on? If you're choosing a button fly, cut the closure edges with your basic seam allowance, without outlets. Do you want to extend or reshape the fly shield into an additional button support?

Center-Back and Vertical Seams: Do you want to add outlets, as shown in the drawing at left, to allow for future expansion in these areas?

Cuffs: Do you want to add extra length for cuffs? Many patterns and textbooks suggest shaping the side seams so that folded-back cuffs or simple hem facings will match the taper, as shown in the drawing below. Obviously, you can't add shaping unless you know exactly where your hem should be, so don't add this feature without careful testing.

I always prefer to be able to establish the hem length when I'm trying on the finished pants. Also, I like to angle my hems so they're slightly longer in back and prefer to set the angle by eye and feel while I'm forming the hem, so I skip this shaping idea. I can always unpick the side seams inside the hem to allow the hem facing to lie as smoothly as possible against the pant legs while I'm hemming them.

Waistband: Do you want a separate waistband or would you prefer a cut-on band, as shown in the drawing below? If you prefer a separate waistband, do you want it to extend beyond the closure edges, either as an overlap or an underlap? Do you want to shape it in any way?

CUT-ON WAISTBAND

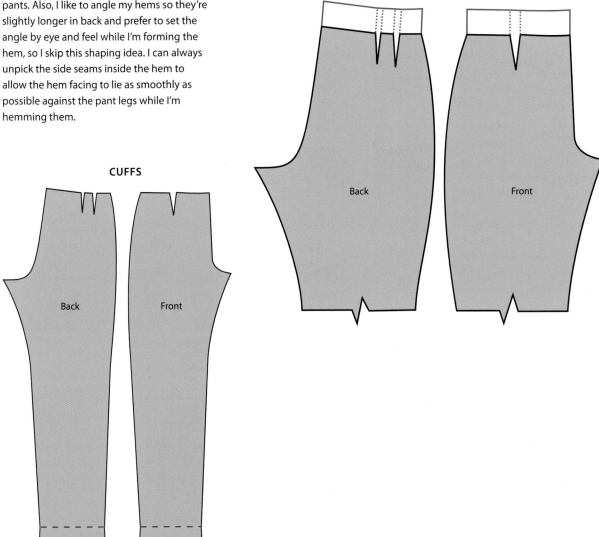

CUFFS

ADDING A CUT-ON WAISTBAND

If you want a cut-on waistband, all you have to do is trace the top edges of your front and back pattern pieces. Next, shift the traced lines up by the width you want (I go for 2 inches [5.1 cm], but 1½ inches [3.8 cm] would do nicely, too). Then draw lines straight down to the old waistline. "Straight down" means perpendicular to the waist edge. In front, this will be parallel to the grain line of the pattern piece; in back, it won't be.

An interesting option to consider is to use a half-band: an add-on band in front or back and a cut-on extension of the same width on the other side. This variation allows you, for example, to ease the back onto a waistband while keeping the fronts smooth, or vice versa.

PIECING THE FORK

To get more garment out of less yardage when laying out your pattern pieces, let the back crotch curve hang off a selvage edge by an inch or two (2.5 to 5.1 cm).

Cut out the back pattern. Piece a selvage scrap onto the cut piece, right sides together, to get the extra room that you need to cut out the full pattern shape. Press open the seam allowances, then put the pattern back and cut the fork.

STAYING THE FORK

To reinforce the front crotch curve (also a fork in tailoring parlance), cut two 6- to 8-inch (15.2 to 20.3 cm) squares of lining fabric. Fold them on the bias, then press the folds, stretching them tautly, as shown in the drawing below.

Place one stretched piece (stay) on the wrong side of each cut-out front and trim the piece's edges to match the front outline. Overcast-stitch each stay in place and include it in the leg and crotch seams that cross it.

STAYING THE FORK

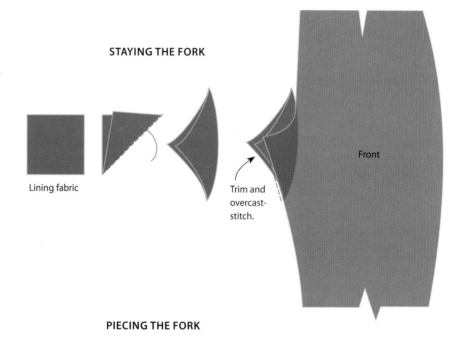

Lining fabric

Front

Trim and overcast-stitch.

PIECING THE FORK

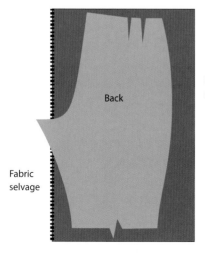

Back

Fabric selvage

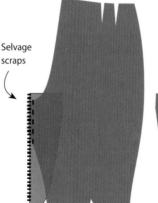

Selvage scraps

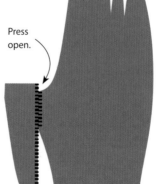

Press open.

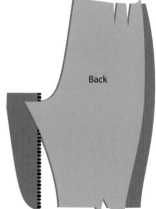

Back

C H A P T E R   F O U R
POCKETS

Making pockets is the fun part of making pants: They're fun to use, fun to design, fun to choose fabrics for, and fun to make. Well, they're fun to make if you know they're going to be struggle-free and great looking, so that's what this chapter's about. The three basic styles described here—on-seam, slant, and welt—allow a wide range of design variations once you get the basics down. The most basic feature they all share is a pocket bag, so we'll cover that first.

BAG BASICS

All pocket bags for the pockets I'll be discussing can be made in one of (at least) three ways. The three options are shown in the drawing below. Note that options **A** and **B** can be used for either front or back pockets, although I prefer the side-fold pocket (**A**) for front pockets. The bottom-fold pocket (**B**) is my choice for back pockets. I don't think I've ever used the two-piece pocket (**C**). I like at least one fold in my pockets, because a fold is generally less likely to spring a leak than a seam (or so I like to think). A joining seam is less bulky if overcast, not turned, but I prefer turning. I wouldn't recommend the top-fold pocket (**D**). This style doesn't allow you to extend the bag to the waist, to get caught in to finish the waistband.

POCKET-BAG BASICS

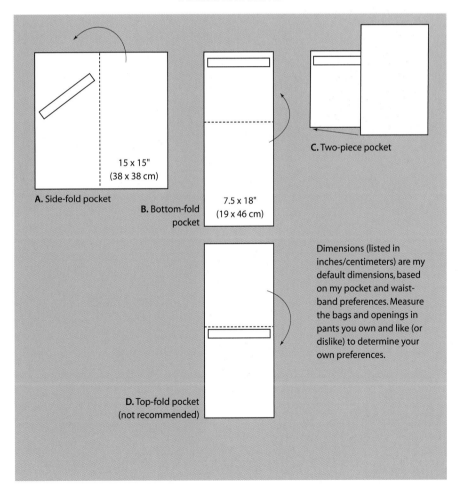

A. Side-fold pocket

15 x 15"
(38 x 38 cm)

B. Bottom-fold pocket

7.5 x 18"
(19 x 46 cm)

C. Two-piece pocket

D. Top-fold pocket
(not recommended)

Dimensions (listed in inches/centimeters) are my default dimensions, based on my pocket and waistband preferences. Measure the bags and openings in pants you own and like (or dislike) to determine your own preferences.

TURNED POCKET BAGS

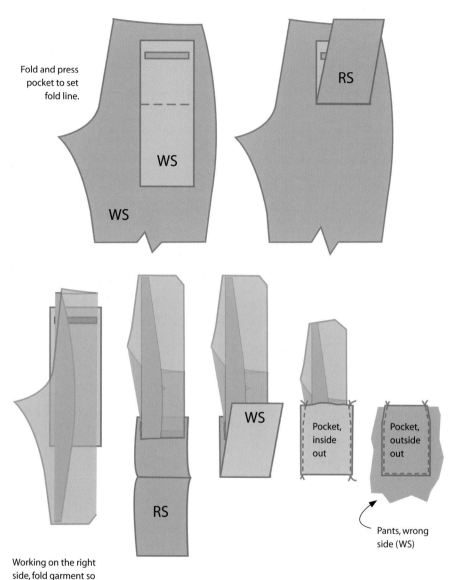

Fold and press pocket to set fold line.

WS

WS

RS

Working on the right side, fold garment so you can refold the pocket around it on the fold line.

RS

WS

Pocket, inside out

Pocket, outside out

Pants, wrong side (WS)

TURNED POCKET BAGS

All three recommended bag types can be turned, so their seamed edges are double-stitched and all the raw edges enclosed. With the pocket turned inside out, as shown in the drawing at left, align its edges and stitch the open sides with a ¼-inch (6 mm) seam allowance. It's traditional to taper the seams above the pocket mouth, at least for back pockets, so the bag gets narrower at the waistline, but the tapering isn't critical. Trim the seam allowances, if you like, and clip the corners. Then turn the bag right side out again.

Now stitch again, with a narrow seam allowance, around all edges—including the fold, if it's at the bottom, as it is here. I don't bother to stitch the vertical, side folds on front-pocket bags.

SHAPING SIDE-FOLD, FRONT-POCKET BAGS

Here's my current strategy for stitching side-fold, front-pocket bags: The pocketing starts out as a simple rectangle (I always cut pocket bags as rectangles and trim them to my stitching as I go) and isn't shaped at the bottom edge until it's stitched. Because my front pockets are my coin pockets, I shape the bag bottom as a curve that slants down toward center front, so the coins will roll toward a single point at the bottom. The forward corner is curved upward, so lint and other little things won't have a corner to collect in.

The rearward edge is curved, too: out, and back in toward the opening to create a little corral for coins to get trapped in when I'm sitting down. After trimming the seam, I turn the pocket right side out again and topstitch the curve. Then I add a little angled line of stitches as a gate for this corral to keep the coins from rolling out, as shown in the photo below. Works like a charm!

Trim the pocket bag to follow your stitching line before turning. This curve is designed to roll coins forward and keep them from spilling out.

ON-SEAM POCKETS

This classic front-pocket style is the least obtrusive way to incorporate pockets into the front of your pants. The pocket mouth is placed directly into the side seam. Adding an ultra-flat, cut-on rather than seamed-on, pocket facing was standard procedure in the heyday of hand-tailored pants—and it's a great idea still.

Add an outlet (extra seam-allowance width) at the pocket-mouth markings on your pant-front pattern, as shown in the drawing below left. The clippings should be single-line scissor cuts. (I've spread the openings in the drawings so you can see them more clearly.)

With the right side up, position the cut-out pant fronts over the front pocketing squares, as shown in the drawing below at right. The pocket should extend about $3/4$ inch (1.9 cm) above the pants at the top, so it can either get covered by or become the band finish. Baste the layers together.

On-seam pockets are classics—and the least obtrusive style of pocket.

ADDING THE OUTLET

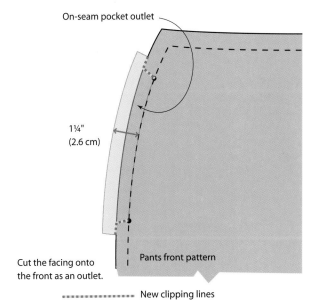

On-seam pocket outlet

1¼"
(2.6 cm)

Cut the facing onto the front as an outlet.

Pants front pattern

New clipping lines

ON-SEAM POCKET BAG PLACEMENT

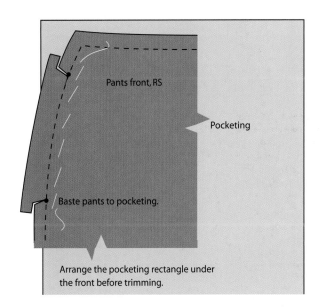

Pants front, RS

Pocketing

Baste pants to pocketing.

Arrange the pocketing rectangle under the front before trimming.

ON-SEAM POCKET BAG SHAPING

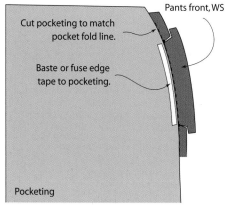

Cut pocketing to match pocket fold line.

Baste or fuse edge tape to pocketing.

Pants front, WS

Pocketing

A. Trim pocketing to match outlet fold line. Then reinforce.

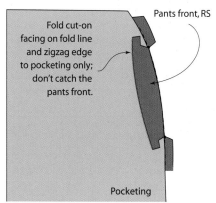

Fold cut-on facing on fold line and zigzag edge to pocketing only; don't catch the pants front.

Pants front, RS

Pocketing

B. Fold outlet over pocket and secure the raw edge.

Fold pocketing to extend beyond side-seam allowance.

Pants front

Pocketing

Slip facing between pocketing layers, aligning edges.

C. Fold pocketing. Then insert facing.

Secure inner edges of pocket facing to pocketing with zigzag stitch.

Pants front

Leave about 1" (2.5 cm) of lower edge of facing unstitched.

Pocketing

D. Fine-tune the positioning of the facing before securing the inner pocketing layer.

Trim the pocketing edge to match the pant-front fold line at the pocket mouth, as shown in drawing **A.** Then reinforce the opening on the pocketing with either hand-basted-in or fused-on stay tape to keep the pocket edge from stretching during wear. You could reinforce the pant front instead, but I think putting the tape on the pocketing makes the finished edge smoother. Fold the outlets to the wrong side and zigzag them to the pocketing, as shown in drawing **B.** Fold the fronts out of the way so they don't get caught in the stitching.

With stiffer fabrics, it may not be possible to press a curve into the front facing's pocket-mouth edge when folding the facing to the inside, so the finished fold line may need to be straighter than shown in the drawing. (Your pattern may not be as curved as shown here, either.)

Fold the pocketing to its intended shape along the folded edge, and allow the open side to extend beyond the side seam allowance so it can later cover and finish the completed side seam. Then position the pocket facing between the pocketing layers so it's aligned with the pant-front side seam, as shown in drawing **C.** Zigzag the inner edges of the facing to the pocketing. When stitching the facing in place, leave 1 inch (2.5 cm) or so unstitched at the bottom edge, as shown in drawing **D**, so you can fold the pocketing out of the way and catch both fronts and facings when stitching the side seams. It's not necessary to catch the top edge of either the cut-on or the inserted facing when securing it to the pocketing.

Now you're ready to stitch closed the bottom edge of the pocketing, as described on page 51. From the front, everything should then look like the photo at right.

Next, make about a 1-inch (2.5 cm) clip just into the layer of the pocketing next to the pant fabric, right below the pocket mouth, as shown in the photo at far right. This clip will enable you to fold the pocketing layers completely out of the way when making the side seam. The clip will be concealed and protected when you cover the completed side seam with the remaining pocketing that extends beyond the facings above the clip.

Finally, before you sew the side seams, topstitch the edge of the pocket mouth, catching and securing the reinforcing tape there. After the side seams are completed and covered with the pocketing, make bar tacks at each end of the pocket mouth through all the layers.

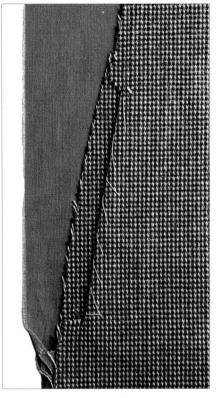

The facing is zigzag-stitched in place, and the front side seams are aligned.

Clip the pocketing fabric just below the pocket mouth. Topstitch the mouth edge.

Leather is a popular piping choice, but Ultrasuede or other synthetics would work just as well.

LEATHER PIPING

Okay, let's make another on-seam pocket, this time adding flat (not corded) piping to the pocket mouth. Leather is a common choice. In fact, I don't think I've ever seen anything besides leather used as a pocket piping—but why not? Certainly Ultrasuede or other synthetic leathers would work well, too. This technique works best on pocket-mouths that are straight or only very slightly curved.

The first step is to create the piping. For the pants shown in the photo at left, I selected a thin section of a soft leather skin and cut two rectangular strips from it, about 1 inch (2.5 cm) longer than the pocket mouth and 1 inch (2.5 cm) wide, aiming for a scant (slightly smaller than) ¼-inch (6 mm) piping. Leather glues well, so I used ordinary glue stick to hold the piping together while I folded each strip in half lengthwise, with wrong sides together.

Before stitching, I fused a stabilizing strip of interfacing along the pocket mouth on the wrong side of the pants. I also marked the upper and lower ends of the pocket mouth with dots, to guide me as I stitched. If your machine is skipping stitches on your sample (you ARE making a sample first, right?), install a leather needle.

To make sure that the folded edge of the piping fell exactly on the side-seam line after turning, I confirmed that my folded leather strip was exactly twice the width I wanted to show. Then I aligned its raw edges along the seam line on the garment's right side and stitched exactly through the center of the strip, as shown in drawing **A**.

To finish the ends of the piping, I first clipped only the pant seam allowance (without cutting the piping), cutting exactly to the ends of my previous stitching line, as shown in drawing **B**. Next, I turned the piping to the wrong side and pressed open the fabric side of the seam from the right side.

A. Postion piping along seamline, fold toward pants, then stitch from dot to dot through center of piping.

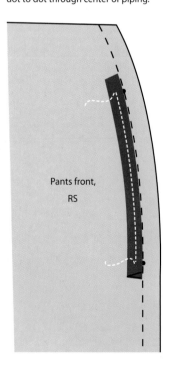

Pants front,
RS

B. From WRONG SIDE, and without cutting piping, clip pants as shown, to each end of stitching.

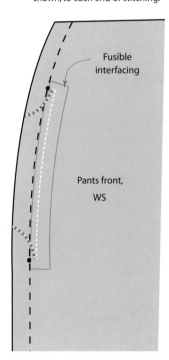

Fusible interfacing

Pants front,
WS

Form the piping by folding and gluing the leather strips in half lengthwise, right sides together.

With that looking okay, I tucked the clipped seam-allowance ends to the wrong side, then folded back the pant fronts at each end, as shown in the photo below at left, exposing the clipped seam allowances. I stitched straight across them and across each end of the piping, catching just the ends of the seam that joined the piping to the pants. With the pant front folded back into position and pressed, these tiny seams create a nice, square corner for the piping. I clipped the piping strip at each end to reduce its bulk a bit, using a really sharp scissors and cutting at an angle rather than straight down, to taper the edge a little.

Next, I needed to re-stitch the original piping seam to add the pocketing layer to it. I arranged the pocketing under the pants, just as I would for a normal on-seam pocket. Then I lifted the pocket-mouth edge of the pants so I could fold the pocketing forward to line up with that original piping seam, as shown in drawing **C**. Then I pinned it in place and opened the layers to expose the seam. Next I stitched directly on top of the original piping seam line.

From here on out, the process for making the pocket is the same as for unpiped, on-seam pockets. Attach the facings to the pocketing, sew the pocket bag closed, topstitch if desired, and complete the side seam. And by all means, make a complete sample before working on your garment!

Notice the ripples on the mouth that was not interfaced (in front) and the flatness of the one that was interfaced (in back). Clearly, it was helpful to have the pant front stabilized against stretching while attaching the leather strip.

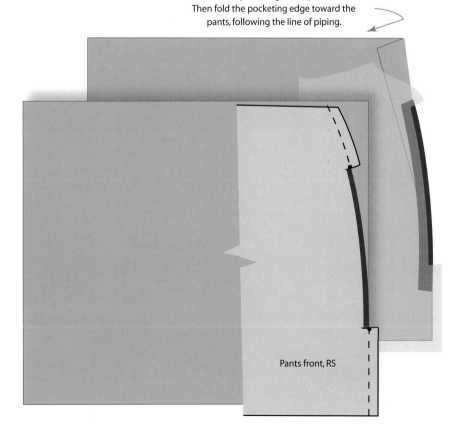

C. Position pocketing under pants front. Then fold the pocketing edge toward the pants, following the line of piping.

Pants front, RS

Fold the clipped seam allowances over the piping at each end. Stitch and trim.

Fold to right side and press the ends of the mouth to form a neat corner.

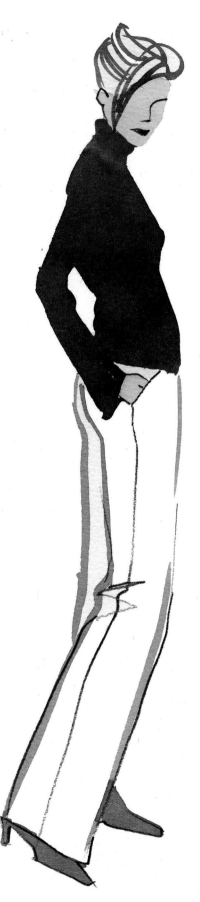

SLANT-FRONT POCKETS

I'm calling a slant-front pocket any front-pocket mouth that starts away from the side seam at the top and ends in the side seam at the bottom, regardless of how its mouth is shaped. As you can see in the drawing below, there are virtually endless possibilities for shaping the mouth, and this construction process can accommodate them all.

The key point with all slanted pockets is that the body-side facing is visible from the outside AND it also forms a portion of both the side and waist seamlines. The pant front needs to be cut away in these areas to create the pocket mouth shape.

There's nothing new about the slant-front style, of course; it's everywhere, from jeans to tuxedos. My tweaks do away with a second facing inside the mouth (never missed it). I also adapt the style to pants with a cut-on band, which would normally close the pocket top. The idea would work equally

SLANT-FRONT POCKET STYLES

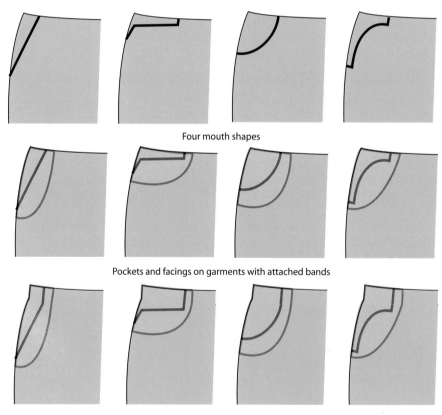

Four mouth shapes

Pockets and facings on garments with attached bands

Pockets and facings on garments with cut-on bands

well with an attached band, as a way to close the pocket mouth below the band/garment seam. This slant-front method lets you end your pocket wherever you want, without making a welt or crossing seam.

I make my version of slant-front pockets with the help of two-part seams on both the front and the facing. The portion of these seams that comes together to join the front to the facing is indicated in red on the drawing at left—where the cut-on band is. The facing is secured to the pocket along the curved portion of the facing seam. The front is joined to the pocketing fabric along the seam. I omit the extra facing in this seam: The pocketing comes right to the edge of the pocket mouth on the inside.

You can make the seam joining the front to the facing either quite noticeable, by not covering it with a belt loop or by topstitching it. Or you can conceal it completely under a loop, as it is in the photo below. The seam will also virtually disappear, even if topstitched, when sewn in a textured or patterned fabric.

TWO-PART SEAMS

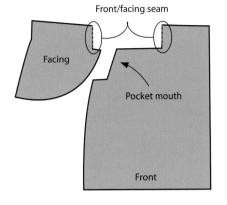
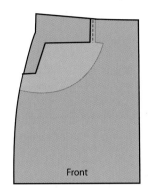

Front/facing seam

Facing

Pocket mouth

Front

Front

CUTTING THE POCKETING FABRIC

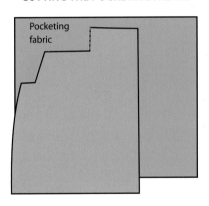

Pocketing fabric

1. Position front over pocketing fabric.

Conceal the seam above your pocket with a belt loop. Or, if you prefer, you can show it off with topstitching.

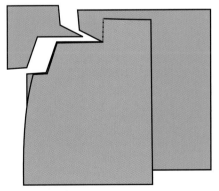

2. Trim away pocketing along pocket-mouth edges.

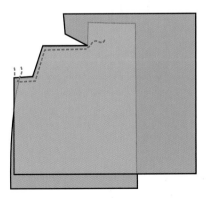

3. Reposition pocketing over front, then stitch pieces together along pocket-mouth edges.

MAKING THE SLANT-FRONT POCKET

To make the pocket, start by stitching the pocket-mouth seam. The pocketing should be garment side up if your pocketing has a right and a wrong side. Most pocketing fabric is the same on both sides, but if yours isn't the same, and you've got a preference for which side goes against your hand inside the pocket or is visible from the inside of the garment (the garment side), make your choice now.

As you can see in the drawing below, the patterns I've provided for these slant pockets have very explicit markings that show exactly where to start and stop your stitches (at the dots) and where to clip to them (at the dots). You'll find full-size marked patterns for a variety of pocket shapes on the companion DVD.

STITCHING THE FACING/FRONT SEAM

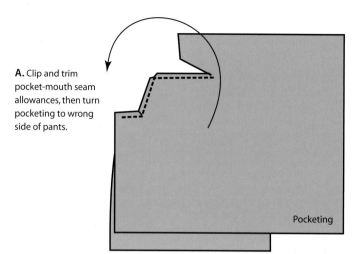

A. Clip and trim pocket-mouth seam allowances, then turn pocketing to wrong side of pants.

Pocketing

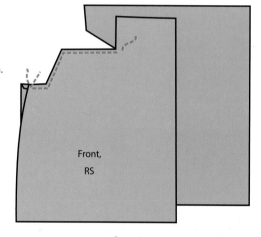

B. Topstitch the pocket-mouth seam.

Front, RS

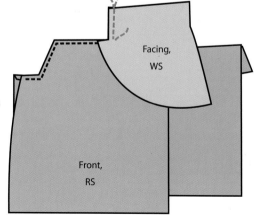

C. Fold pocketing out of the way, then stitch facing to fronts, right sides together.

Facing, WS

Front, RS

SAMPLE PATTERN FOR SLANT-FRONT POCKET

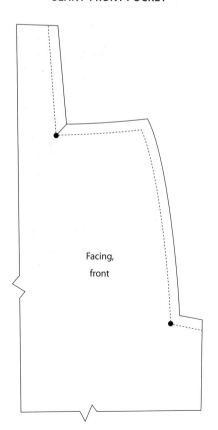

Facing, front

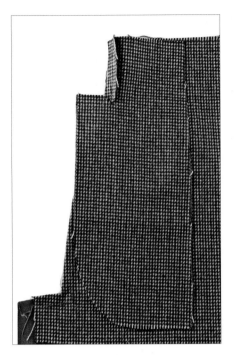

Join the facing to the front, right sides together. Press open the seam allowances.

Turn the facing right side up, tucking the corner inside the front.

Here, the cut-on band is folded down to show the pocketing fabric behind it.

After joining the facing to the front, I press open the clipped seam allowances and turn the facing right side up, tucking the upper corner of its curved edge underneath the pant front. I leave the top corner of the pocketing rectangle (the section that's closer to the side seam) untrimmed until after I've topstitched the facing/front seam, stitching through the pocketing there as a way of reinforcing the seam. (If I want this stitching to be less visible, I stitch it once in the ditch of the seam rather than twice: once on each side of the seam. Is either really necessary? Probably not, but I like the way it looks.)

In the photo at right, you can see the facing again, from the inside of the pocket. In the photo at far right, I've folded the pocketing in half to form the pocket. In the photo below at left, I'm ready to secure the inner edge of the facing to the pocketing. Remember to stop stitching about 1 inch (2.5 cm) short of the lower edge of the facing.

From here on out, completing the slant pocket is just the same as completing the on-seam pocket (page 53). The steps include clipping the inner layer of the turned bag just below the pocket mouth to allow the pocket to be folded back and to avoid getting it caught in the side seam.

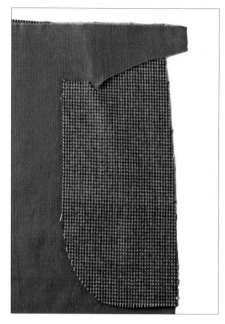

After the facing is joined to the front and turned, here is how it looks on the inside of the pocket.

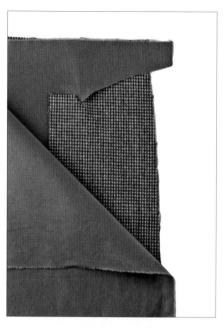

To form the pocket, fold the pocket fabric over the facing.

Turn the pocket to the right side and secure the inner edge of the facing to the pocketing with zigzag stitching.

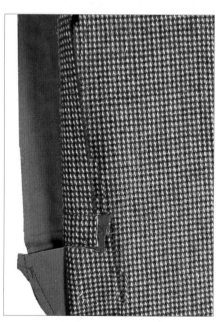

Clip the inside pocketing layer just below the pocket mouth.

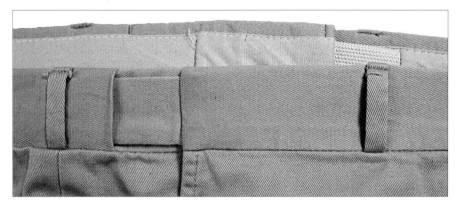

These expanding-waist pocket details are from a garment by Orvis, discussed in the pants tour, page 18.

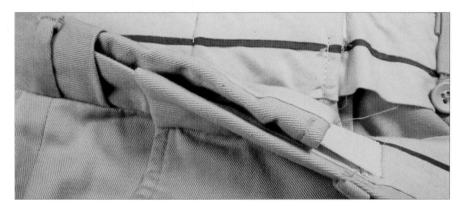

These expanding-waist pocket details are from a garment by Orvis, discussed in the pants tour, page 18.

EXPANDING-WAIST POCKETS

Here's an interesting option for slant pockets: expandability. Remember that expanding waistline in the Orvis men's pants in the tour? You can see it again in the top two photos at left.

The two photos below show a stripped-to-basics variation on this idea applied to a cut-on waistband; an add-on band would work just as well.

This waist treatment is essentially an elaboration on a slant pocket, with the waistband split, not joined, at the top of the pocket mouth. The pocketing is simply stitched to the pocket mouth all the way to the top of the band, which has been finished with a piece of petersham ribbon. Even more significant, the facing underneath has also been extended to the top of the band and forward, too, deep into the pocket. Most significant, the pocket itself has been divided at its forward fold, just like the pocket on the Orvis pants.

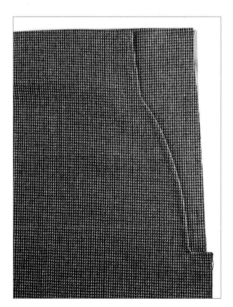

This slant-top pocket is not joined to the facing at the waist.

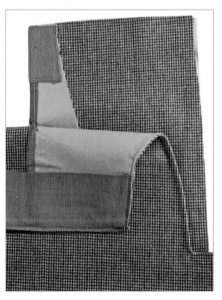

Here, the pocket is folded down to reveal the layers of the split pocketing.

MECHANICS OF THE EXPANDING POCKET

If you use this basic expandable-pocket structure, there are a lot of ways to make a working pair of adjustable pants. The most straightforward method, I suppose, would be simply to add a belt and belt loops to hold the layers together; loosen your belt, and the pants will loosen, too. But it then becomes somewhat troublesome to shrink the waistline back to normal without elastic to pull it in.

SECURING OPTIONS FOR EXPANDABLE POCKETS

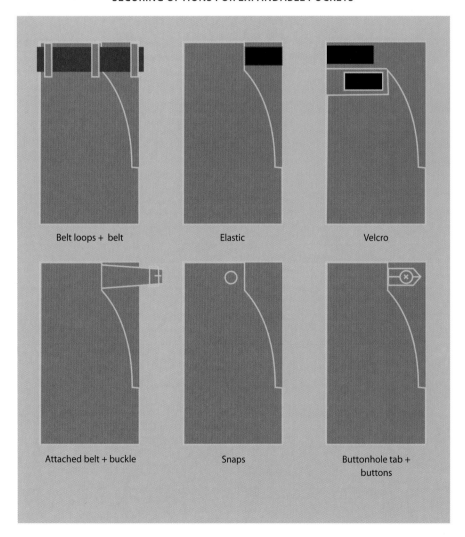

Belt loops + belt

Elastic

Velcro

Attached belt + buckle

Snaps

Buttonhole tab + buttons

If you add elastic from the side seam to the front, you don't need to cover it, as in the Orvis version, as long as you add the belt loops and belt. Or perhaps you wouldn't mind the look of a simple, visible elastic insert (I don't). Or you might consider placing Velcro between the band layers and doing without a belt altogether.

Or add your own self-fabric belt; the buckle could be attached to the side seam or pants back with a folded strip of elastic, and a single, visible snap cover could connect to several hidden snap bases inside, just as a buttonhole tab could access multiple buttons.

An issue that must be addressed when you're considering adding an expanding-waist pocket to pants is the inherent distortion that will occur when the pocket is actually expanded. There's no way to avoid some distortion, but I can vouch for the fact that the spreading pocket is quite unobtrusive in use, despite how odd it may look when stretched while laid flat. Carefully choose what your undistorted waist circumference will be so you can be comfortable and minimize the distortions needed to get to your maximum change in circumference. Obviously, you'll need to experiment, but there's a lot of room for interesting innovations.

POCKET WITH BELT LOOPS AND ELASTIC

Here's one way to achieve a belt-loops-plus-elastic version. First, I cut two equal-length pieces of elastic, one to position in front underneath the bands and one to position in the rear on top. Next, I started with this basic structure: an open-top slant pocket on a cut-on waistband, with a pocket bag divided for a few inches (a half-dozen centimeters) along the pocket fold. The open edges of the pocket bag are covered with a rayon seam binding. The photo sequence on the next two pages shows the construction steps.

MAKING A BELT-LOOPS-PLUS-ELASTIC EXPANDING POCKET

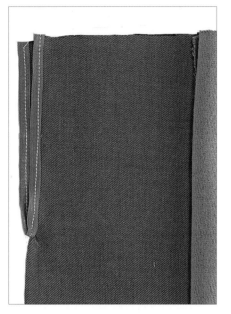

1. I enclosed the split at the fold at the front of the pocket with rayon seam binding.

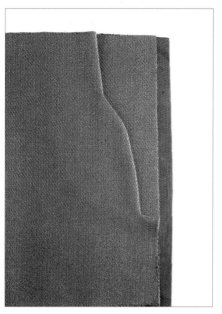

2. To create an opening in the front/pocketing seam, where I'll insert one end of the rear elastic, I stitched the seam all the way to the top and pressed thoroughly.

3. Then I carefully ripped the seam, as shown, to establish a clean edge for securing the elastic. Then I stitched the side seam.

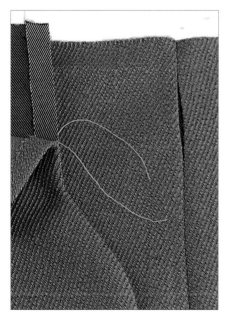

4. At the side seam, I switched to a basting stitch where I wanted a slot for inserting the other end of the rear elastic. I pressed the side seam open to keep it as flat as possible. Then I picked the basted stitches to open the seam slot, as shown.

5. I inserted the rear elastic into the slot. The elastic was long enough to cover the gap between the pocket top and the side seam, plus the ¼-inch (6.4 cm) seam allowances at each end.

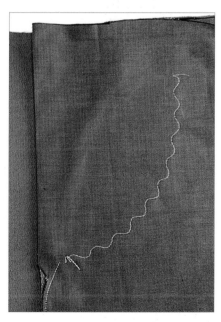

6. After securing the rear elastic between the pocket top and side seam, I folded and pressed the pocketing edge to cover the side-seam seam allowances.

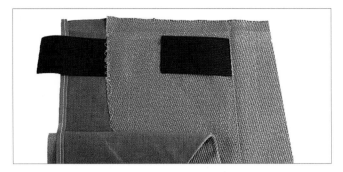

7. I topstitched the side seam to further secure the elastic and also to catch the folded pocketing underneath. Then I zigzagged the front piece of elastic in place under the forward edge of the pocket facing.

8. To hold the petersham to the top seam allowance of the extended band, I ironed on a length of Extra Fine Fusing Tape.

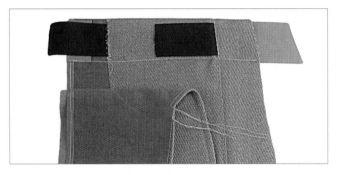

9. After pulling off the tape's paper backing, I fused on the petersham and edge-stitched it just outside the top-edge fold line. I turned the petersham to the wrong side, wrapped it around the forward edge of the pocket split, and topstitched through all layers to secure it at its bottom edge.

10. I also applied petersham to the front section of the waistband in the same way, allowing enough extra length in back to wrap over and into the open front/facing seam where the rear elastic will be secured.

11. Stitching across this open seam from the outside, without catching the underlapping facing layers below, I secured the free end of the rear elastic to the front, along with the folded seam allowances of front, pocketing, and petersham. I zigzag-stitched the front elastic to secure it to the outer layer's petersham, still unattached at its bottom edge. I transferred the stitching line from the under layer to the front with chalk and a ruler, then added the waist-level topstitching along the marked line to secure the bottom edge of the over layer's petersham.

12. Finally, I added belt loops to conceal the elastic stitching; a belt will conceal the elastic itself. With this variation, you easily gain 2 inches (5 cm) or more of temporary additional length on each side.

DOUBLE WELTS

Welts allow you to place a pocket mouth anywhere you want within the middle of a pattern piece—they're based on slashes made through the fabric and don't require access to a nearby seam line. Welts are typically used for back pockets in pants, but are often found in front, too.

There are lots of ways to make welts and lots of ways to vary them. I've become fond of a simple approach that has many virtues: It provides very flat, soft results; it's easy to remember how to do it; it requires minimal marking; and it can be easily adapted to produce every welt variation I'm ever likely to need, including single, double, curved, and flapped styles. This method is also the method likely to be used by custom tailors, because it allows you to press open the welt/garment seam allowances, resulting in as smooth a transition as possible from garment face to welt.

PARTS FOR A BASIC DOUBLE-WELT POCKET

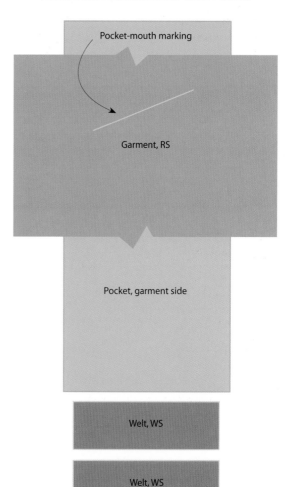

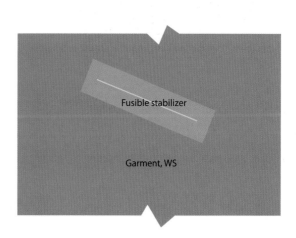

WELT POCKET STYLES

Double

Curved

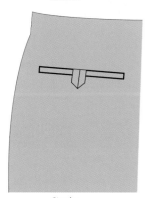

Single

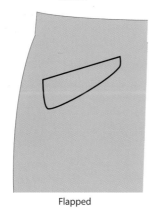

Flapped

DOUBLE-WELT LAYOUT

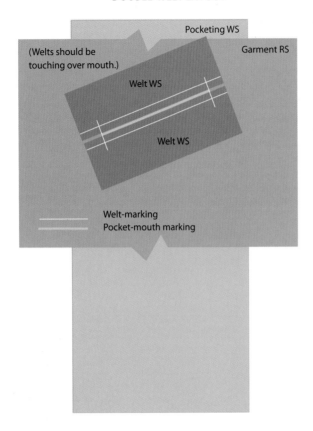

Pocketing WS

Garment RS

(Welts should be touching over mouth.)

Welt WS

Welt WS

Welt-marking
Pocket-mouth marking

DOUBLE WELTS (CROSS-SECTION VIEW)

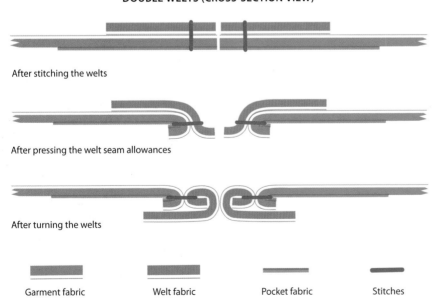

After stitching the welts

After pressing the welt seam allowances

After turning the welts

Garment fabric   Welt fabric   Pocket fabric   Stitches

Usually, it's wise to add a fusible interfacing on the wrong side of the garment fabric, with its stable direction in line with the pocket mouth and covering it: for example, whenever your pocket mouth is at an angle to the garment grain and/or when the pocket crosses a dart, as is likely for back pockets. The interfacing also helps to support those tiny triangles that plague most folks when slashing at the end of pocket openings, especially on likely-to-fray fabrics.

To make double welts, start by marking the position and length of the pocket mouth on the right side of the pants. Cut your welts about 1 ½ inches (3.8 cm) longer than the pocket opening, so you'll have ¾ inch (1.9 cm) to turn inside at each end. When marking the welts, simply draw a line parallel to one long edge—exactly one welt-width away from the edge, or half the size of the whole pocket. So, for example, if your pocket mouth is to be ½-inch (1.3 cm) wide, with two ¼-inch (6.4 mm) welts, mark each welt piece ¼ inch (6.4 mm) from the edge. Then simply place the welts so they're flush with and parallel to the pocket marking, and just touching one another. Chalk across the welts at each end of the opening, to mark where you'll stop stitching, now or—if the pocket's curved—after basting.

The three diagrams at left show a cross-section, or cutaway, view of a typical double-welt structure. You can see how the seam allowances lie after stitching the welts and cutting through all layers, after pressing the seam allowances open, and after turning the welts to the wrong side.

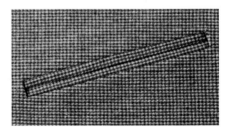

In a double-welt pocket, the two welts are flush with and parallel to the pocket opening. Their edges just touch each other.

ATTACHING THE WELTS

When applying welts, it's best to baste them in place before stitching through them, especially if they're curved. (I highly recommend that you try hand-basting with tailor's basting cotton.) Curved welts are no different from straight welts, except that they must be cut on the bias in order to curve. Simply pin the welt along the pocket-mouth mark so that at the stitching line it is neither stretched nor eased. Let the edges deform as they will, and they'll take the curve beautifully. Then baste by hand.

One great advantage of thread-basting over pinning is that you can baste exactly on the stitching line, then machine-stitch over the basting with no worries about shifting or distorting the layers while you pull out the pins. If you happen to catch a basting thread with your machine needle, the thread will break or clip away easily. Reinforce the end markings before you stitch, to be sure you hit them, and don't stitch across the ends—you need to leave them open for proper turning.

Carefully lift the welts and cut along the opening line through all the other layers, angling off to clip to the ends of each stitching line about ½ inch (1.3 cm) from the ends of the mouth. It's critical that you clip ALL the way to the ends of the stitching, or you won't be able to turn the welts fully to the wrong side. Go back and clip farther if you're having trouble doing this. I like to use a rotary cutter for most of the single-line cuts since it makes such a clean, sharp cut, and I use trimming scissors for the clipping.

Here's the magic moment: pressing open the welt/garment seam allowances. Photograph 3 shows the seam from the back, which is, of course, where you do the pressing. (The drawing on the facing page shows the cross-section view.) This pressing step is what ensures a flat, professional effect when your welts are fully turned. Don't skip it!

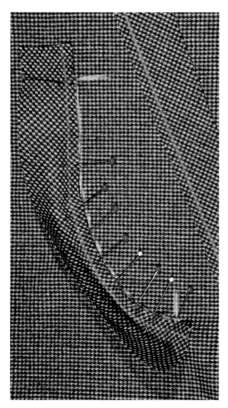

1. Pin and then baste the welts to either side of the pocket-mouth marking line.

2. Stitch on the welt marking lines, end to end, but do not stitch across the welt ends.

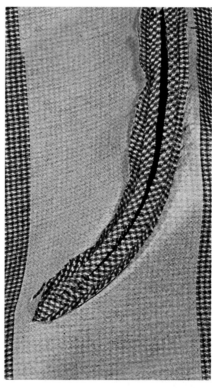

3. After cutting through all layers (without catching the welts), press the garment seam allowance away from the welts.

The welts are pressed and turned to the wrong side. Notice the lower welt was cut wider and on the selvage.

Hold the end triangles in place with a dab of glue.

After the welt is turned and pressed, it should look, from the wrong side, something like the sample shown in the top photo above. I used a wider strip for the lower welt on this back pocket. I cut it on the selvage so I didn't have to turn its edge under when securing it to the pocketing—flatness!

Here's a useful tip for managing those little triangles at each end of the welt. They need to be pressed fully open to ensure square, straight ends for your pocket mouth. Dig a tiny dab of glue from a glue-stick with a pin, then slip the pin under the triangle for precise glue delivery. (I chose purple glue so it would be easier to see in the photo.)

SECURING THE WELTS

After the welts are formed and pressed, the most elegant plan for securing them is to lift the garment fabric at the welt edges in order to stitch all around the pocket opening, as shown in cross-section in the drawing at right. Both welts and the end triangles are secured by stitching through the pocketing exactly on top of the pocket/garment seams at top and bottom and across the triangle folds at each end (rather than by stitching in the ditch of the welt/garment seams, which is the more usual method).

Lift the garment away from each edge of the pocket opening, as shown in the drawing and photos at right. Note that you're stitching the welt/garment allowances in place only, and to one layer of pocketing, not closing the pocket. That's fine for now—you'll catch the other side of the pocket in a later step. There's a lot to do first.

Next, turn the whole garment piece to the pocketing side. With the garment folded out of the way, secure the lower edge of the welt piece to the pocket. For the most professional results on the outside of the finished pocket, change the bobbin thread to match the pocketing. Then stitch a straight line from one edge of the pocketing to the other, rather than just across the welt width. The upper welt's raw edge doesn't need to be further secured; it'll never be seen or touched again.

STITCHING THE DOUBLE WELTS (CROSS-SECTION VIEW)

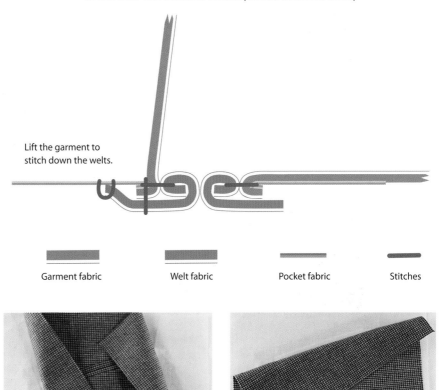

Lift the garment to stitch down the welts.

| Garment fabric | Welt fabric | Pocket fabric | Stitches |

Lift the garment layer to secure the ends (left) and the top and bottom (right) of the welted opening.

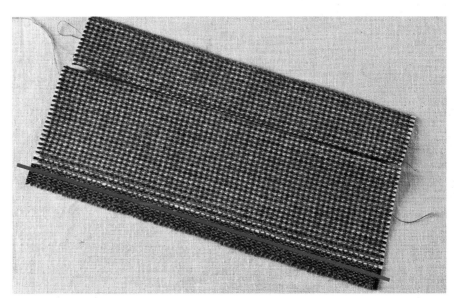

Secure the lower welt's lower edge only to the pocketing. The stitching line is shown in red.

ADDING A FACING

If you're adding a pocket flap, you don't also need a facing (at least that's my opinion; add one if you like), so you can proceed to page 72 to make the flap. If you're not adding a flap, now's the time to position the facing inside the pocket behind your welts.

On the selvage of the fabric, if possible, cut a rectangle the length of the welts and about 2 inches (5.1 cm) wide to make the facing. Position the rectangle face down over the turned welts as shown in the top photo. The selvage edge of the lower welt is toward the bottom of the garment, and the upper, cut edge of the facing extends beyond the welt opening by at least ½ inch (1.3 cm).

Fold the pocketing fabric up over the welts and facing to its finished position. Mark the fold with a crease or with notches. Then pin the top layer of the folded pocketing to the facing, as shown in the bottom photo. (Note: The pocketing in the photo is abnormally shortened in this sample.)

Unfold the pocketing and secure both of the facing's long edges to it. Because this stitching will be on the hidden side of the pocket, it doesn't matter what bobbin thread you use, or whether you stitch all the way to the pocketing edges. Now you're ready to form and turn the bags, as described on page 50. When that's done, proceed with the steps on page 73.

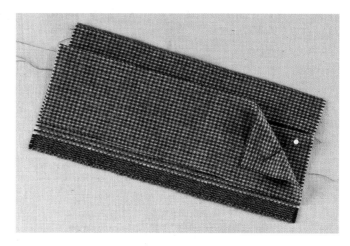

Position the facing face down over the welts on the inside of the pocket. The cut edge of the facing should extend beyond the welt opening by at least ¼ inch (6 mm).

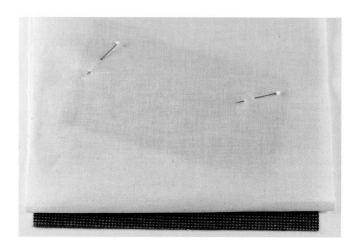

Fold the pocketing over the welts and facing. Pin the pocketing to the facing only.

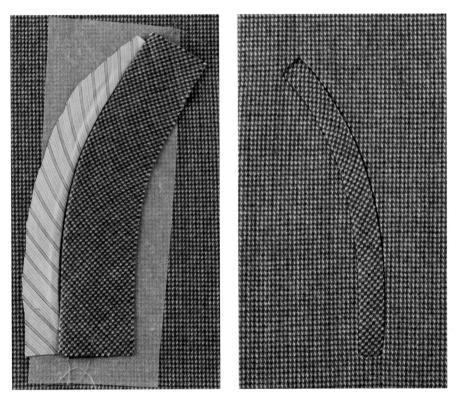

SINGLE WELTS

The trick to adapting the double-welt technique to make a single welt is simply to use a lining-weight fabric for the inner, hidden, welt so it can be folded entirely out of sight when turning the welts.

In the cross-section drawing below, notice that the visible welt's seam allowance can be made wider than half the mouth width, so that it fills and supports more of the welt width when pressed open, avoiding an unevenly filled welt. To provide this wider allowance, simply overlap the welt seam allowances over the pocket-mouth marking line, rather than butting them edge to edge (as you did for the double welt). The overlap will extend the welt's seam-allowance edge all the way to the stitching line for the lining piece.

To form a single welt, use a lining-weight fabric for the inner welt. The fabric will fold out of sight when you turn the welt.

SINGLE WELT (CROSS-SECTION VIEW)

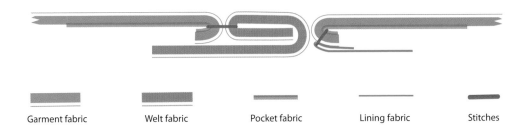

| Garment fabric | Welt fabric | Pocket fabric | Lining fabric | Stitches |

TABS OR FLAPS

You can insert a button tab or a flap to convert a single welt into a tabbed or flapped single-welt pocket. Simply make a single-welt pocket, then slip the completed tab or flap inside before you secure the top edge, as shown in the photos at right. Notice the lining peeking out along the upper edge of the welt opening before the flap and the pocket mouth are secured there. Nothing to worry about. The peeking bit will disappear when you fold down the garment above the pocket and stitch exactly on the garment/pocketing seam. To be sure it's completely out of the way, pull the lining slightly away from the mouth from inside when you fold back the garment to stitch along this seam line. The drawing below shows how it all sits when you're done.

Here are a few tips to remember when adding flaps. Be sure to angle the ends of the pocket mouth so the lower edge is narrower than the open upper edge, ensuring that the flap will fully cover the welt below, as shown in the photos on the facing page. Note that when you cut and clip the opening in a case like this, the little end triangles will slant downward. If you're making men's pants, be sure to measure the wallet that may be slipped into this back pocket before you commit yourself to a pocket-mouth width—you've been warned!

The welt won't be visible under a flap; if your fabric is heavy or thick, don't add unnecessary bulk by using it for the welt. Choose a thin, lightweight fabric in a compatible color, as I've done for the heavy wool pants, whose pocket is shown in the top photo on page 74.

A flap is an optional, last-minute add-on to a single welt opening. Slip the flap in place before securing the top edge.

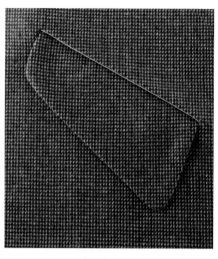

The lining-weight welt will disappear when you stitch the seam to close the pocket.

Fold back the garment to secure the flaps and close the pocket.

SINGLE WELT WITH FLAP (CROSS-SECTION VIEW)

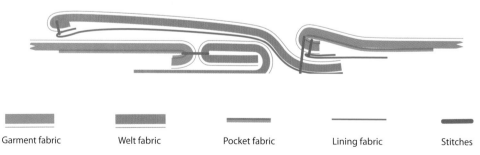

| Garment fabric | Welt fabric | Pocket fabric | Lining fabric | Stitches |

TOPSTITCHING AND MACHINE-TACKING

As explained on page 69, before you turned the pocket you secured all four sides of the pocket mouth (and any flaps or tabs) from underneath the garment fabric. This stitching, however, doesn't close the pocket above the mouth or give the pocket mouth the strength it needs. You still need to stitch around the ends and across the top edge of the mouth through all layers to complete the pocket. Stitch on the garment face as topstitching or stitch out of sight, under the garment layer, by lifting the garment (just as when securing the welts in the first place, as described on page 69). I usually topstitch from the outside, especially if topstitching is part of the design of the garment elsewhere. I'm sure this is a somewhat stronger finish than stitching underneath. Sometimes, however, you might prefer not to have visible topstitching. Just look back at the vintage men's tour garments if you'd like some beautiful confirmation (see pages 24–27).

Notice how the topstitching around the flapped pockets shown on page 74 extends out into a semitriangular point at each end?

Having learned the hard way that the most likely place for my pants to tear was right at the end of the back pockets, I was intrigued to read about a solution in a wonderful old men's tailoring manual (J. E. Liberty's 1933 *Practical Tailoring*, see page 134). In the high-class trade, welted pockets (Liberty calls them jetted) were all finished with D-tacks at the ends. There's an adaptation of the tack diagrams from his book shown in the drawing below. Naturally, I resolved to add something similar to the next pair I made. I've not had a rip since.

Angle the welt ends so the lower edge of the pocket mouth is narrower than the top edge. Notice the lightweight flap lining fabric. When the flap is in place, it will fully cover the welt.

POCKET TACKS FROM J. E. LIBERTY

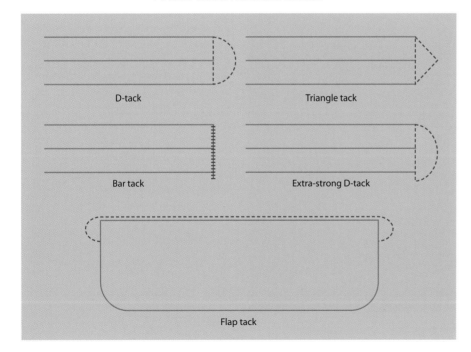

D-tack

Triangle tack

Bar tack

Extra-strong D-tack

Flap tack

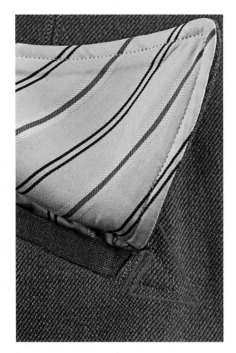

When topstitching, add shaped tacks at the pocket ends for durability and style. Triangles are easier to stitch than curves.

Flap tacks merge with the topstitching above the flap.

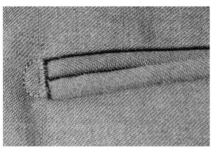

Here's a nice D-tack on a ready-to-wear garment from Ermenegildo Zegna Group.

Of course, my D-tacks are not hand-sewn with invisible pick-stitches, as Liberty describes. Nor are they tiny and rounded, as the D in the name suggests and as the machine-made tacks are on the very high-end contemporary specimens I found. I'm an unrepentant machine-topstitcher and, for better or worse, not at my machine all day every day. So, I quickly observed that a triangle is a much easier shape to stitch accurately and repeatedly than a tiny half-circle, no matter how skillful you are! My topstitching goes through all layers and is added after the pocket is completed inside. I'm rather fond of the effect of these shaped tacks, but a simple bar tack, or even just a couple of rows of straight stitching, positioned right at the welt ends, will look fine, too.

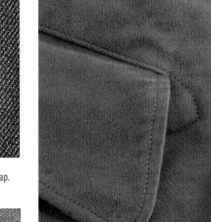

Even a curved triangle is easier to stitch than a half-circle.

ZIPPER POCKETS AND OTHER SECURITY FEATURES

Then there's the welt-less pocket opening, perfect for dropping a zipper into when you feel the need for a security zone in your trousers—or elsewhere. The pocketing should be underneath when you start, just as it would be for any other welt pocket. Because every edge on this opening is intended to be turned out of sight, the facing should be as thin as possible.

To achieve that effect, bring out the lining once again and back your pocket mouth with fusible interfacing, especially if it's off-grain. Then stitch around all four sides of the pocket opening. After cutting through the layers, clipping into the corners, and turning the lining, glue-baste the zipper into position (or use fusing tape, as I did in example E on the facing page). Before lifting the garment fabric to topstitch invisibly around the zipper through the pocketing, I've forced the teeth to join again above the slider to keep the tapes together.

Welts, or a flap, could certainly also be inserted to cover the zipper, if desired, and the ends of the opening could be angled, too. A facing underneath is purely optional, depending on what your pocketing choice is and whether you want to show it off or not. On a vertical or slanted pocket, I'd position the slider at the bottom when closed, rather than at the top—or I'd position it wherever it was less likely to chafe when I passed my hand over it (if on a front-pocket facing, for instance). Or I'd add a welt.

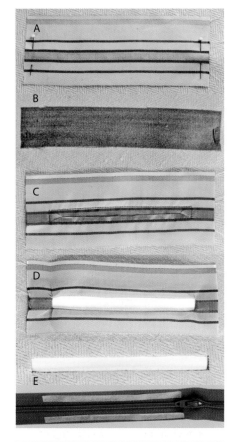

A POCKET WITHIN A POCKET

As I've mentioned, I loved adding a little pouch for a Swiss Army knife inside the front pocket of the first pants I ever made. I've since added many such a patch pocket to my trousers—all variations on the one shown in the Brooks Brothers RTW pants on the tour, shown on page 16, which have the pouch stitched to the inner pocket layer. I've tried curved patches and angled ones, too, and have set them into inner pocketing layers in various places. Although I eventually ditched the knife, I still had the old problem of spilling coins, so I kept the patch idea as the solution.

It turns out that each time I added one of these little patches, I found it was increasingly annoying to have around. My fingers were more likely to snag on it than to find it handy. So, I'm delighted to have hit on the simple idea of merely reshaping the pocket bag and adding a stitched gate to catch errant coins when I'm sitting down. You can see this neat device in the photo below.

To insert a zipper, pin the lining over the mouth on the right side (A). Fuse the mouth on the wrong side (B). Stitch a box around the mouth line. Slash it at center (C). Turn the lining to the wrong side and press on the right side (D). Baste the zipper in position with fusible tape (E). Secure by lifting the garment layer, as for welt openings, and stitching all around (F).

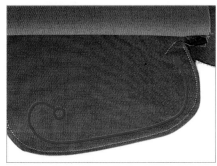

Shape and stitch the pocket bag to reduce the likelihood that coins will roll out.

FLY FRONTS

I've got three goals when making a zipper fly. First, make sure the zipper is positioned well inside the overlap so there's no chance that the zipper is visible and that there's plenty of room for the slider at the top. Second, make sure the overlap topstitching is smooth, unpuckered, and nowhere lumpy. Third, as always, try to keep everything as thin, flat, and flexible as possible. The techniques I'm presenting here meet all these requirements. But if you're still resisting zippers, as I tend to do, feel free to join me as I attempt the long-overdue revival of the wonderful button fly.

ZIPPER-FLY BASICS

I start with the easiest process I know of for taking care of the overlap problem, shown to me first by Sandra Betzina. In this well-known basted-seam approach, the front crotch seam is stitched and the placement of the center-front opening is fixed before the zipper is attached. This process is the exact opposite, incidentally, of the tailor's method described by Stanley Hostek, but it's similar to the couture process described by Claire Shaeffer, in which the zipper is hand-stitched over a basted-closed overlap. It's easy and it works.

One difference between many men's and women's pants patterns is that a women's pattern often has cut-on extensions at the fly opening, rather than separate pieces for the fly facing and shield that are sewn on at the center-front seam line. For years, I ignored the cut-on approach, vaguely assuming it somehow indicated lower standards for women's garments, ignoring what should have been obvious: Cut-ons eliminate the bulk of a seam, and they fold over on a perfectly straight edge. If you want your center-front closure to dip into the crotch curve (as men's pants always did when flies buttoned and for a while even after zippers took over), the facing and shield will need to be stitched on, not folded, to follow the curved opening. If the opening is confined to the straight portion of the seam, however, cut-on extensions make a lot of sense.

So, do men's flies need to open beyond the straight part of the front crotch seam? Well, no; and they haven't done so on most ready-to-wear pants and commercial pant patterns for years. Take a look at the curves I recently traced from a variety of patterns,

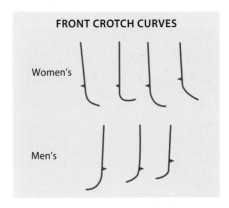

FRONT CROTCH CURVES

Women's

Men's

Modern patterns do not place the zipper bottom into the curved part of the center-front seam.

shown above. Notice that the seams on both men's and women's pants are quite variable in the shape and extent of the curve, but that, in every case, the zipper-end notch is always placed well into the straight portion of the seam, and it could often be moved a bit farther down without entering the curve.

Another common distinction between women's and men's pants has been that men's always have a fly shield—a strip of fabric covering the zipper teeth from the inside and usually extending well below the zipper over the crotch seam. Women's pants often don't, which sort of goes along with having zipper extensions cut-on rather than sewn. I guess the logic for not having cut-on extensions for men was that if you're going to stitch on a shield, and cut it longer than the fly opening to cover it, you might as well do the same with the fly facing, too—saves cutting the fly differently on each side. But I see only benefit in cut-on fly extensions, regardless of whether I'll be adding an extra shield piece or not, as you'll see.

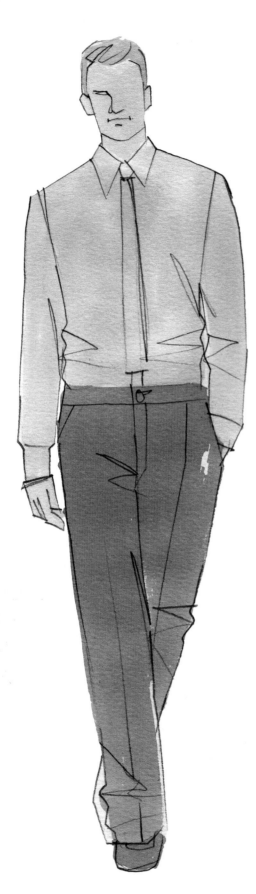

To adapt using cut-on extensions to my gender-free approach for all pants, I start by increasing their width from around 1 inch (2.5 cm) to 2 ½ inches (6.4 cm) from edge to center front, as shown in the drawing at right. I also drop the lower curve of the extensions a good 1 inch (2.5 cm) below the notch or dot so they'll extend well below the zipper tape. This way, the extensions will be easily caught in the fly-front topstitching, which I also want to extend below the zipper, without hitting it.

To use a cut-on underlap extension as a built-in shield, I've experimented with a clever idea from Roberto Cabrera and Patricia Flaherty Meyers' excellent book, *Classic Tailoring Techniques: A Construction Guide for Women's Wear* (see page 133). Their idea is to press under the zipper tape on its center-front side, rather than folding back the fabric that it's attached to, as shown in the sidebar below and drawing **B** on the facing page.

CUT-ON FLY PATTERN

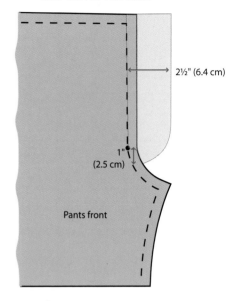

2½" (6.4 cm)

1" (2.5 cm)

Pants front

A cut-on fly extension makes a bulk-free fly on both men's and women's trousers.

PLASTIC vs. METAL ZIPPERS

For me, the important distinction between these two common, flyweight zipper types is the flexibility of the tapes. The metal zippers I've seen have much softer, more fabriclike tapes than plastic zippers, but I've just picked up what I can easily find online. Metal zippers are my zipper of choice when I plan to fold the tape, as for a cut-on waist zipper. In general, a softer and more flexible tape will make any zipper more amenable to experimentation.

If I'm stuck with plastic, I facilitate the pressing of the stiff plastic tape by establishing a crease with a quick press and then applying a length of extra-fine fusing tape inside the fold. A more sustained press makes the fold permanent.

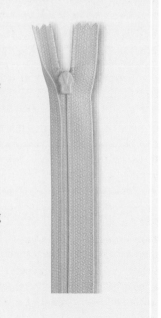

Metal-toothed zippers are usually on flexible cloth tapes, which are easy to stitch down first, then fold onto themselves. The finished effect may be flatter, too, because this method tends to bend the shield piece around the zipper fold a bit and can be pressed to encourage this, shown in **B2** at right. This method seems to be the least-layered way to insert a zipper; but it makes the teeth the most-raised part of the zipper assembly, so it's best with fabrics sturdy enough to lie smoothly over the ridge of the zipper teeth. With very lightweight or flexible fabrics, the risk of raised zipper teeth creating imprints is a risk I prefer not to take, so I revert to an add-on shield, the more common approach—but I still do it with a cut-on extension. Because all the fly methods here can be made with either a right or a left opening, I'll refer to the sides as overlapping or underlapping, not left or right.

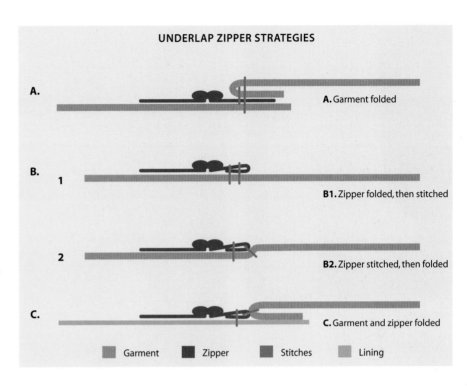

UNDERLAP ZIPPER STRATEGIES

A. Garment folded

B1. Zipper folded, then stitched

B2. Zipper stitched, then folded

C. Garment and zipper folded

Garment   Zipper   Stitches   Lining

CUT-ON-WAIST ZIPPER WITH CUT-ON FLY SHIELD

In this example, I'm working on a sample with a cut-on waistband. To start, I cut the pattern as shown in the drawing on the facing page, marking the zipper stop with an X and clipping both sides to mark the center-front fold lines at the top edge. I'll use strategy **B2**, shown in the drawing above.

Because this opening is for a cut-on, not an attached, waistband, I also positioned the upper zipper stops well below the top of the fly (on an actual garment, this would be about 2 inches (5.1 cm). I'll be able to fold the upper ends of the zipper tape down and under, to create a clean finish.

Finally, I created a new lower stop for the zipper by zigzagging across it. The photo at far right shows how I like to trim the teeth away while leaving a little tape below a thread zipper-stop at the bottom. If your tape seems particularly ravel-prone, you could use a liquid fray-stop product here, but this area will be permanently covered, so don't worry about it.

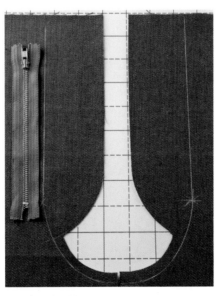

Here's a fly with cut-on extensions, all marked up and ready to go.

Unwanted teeth, either plastic or metal, can be easily cut away. Metal teeth can also be removed individually with nipping pliers.

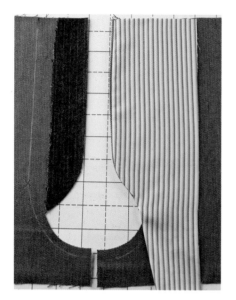

1. The overlap is interfaced, and the underlap is lined.

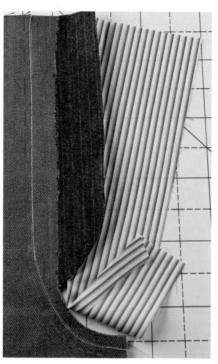

2. The crotch curve is stitched, and the center-front is basted.

3. The zipper is positioned with the teeth on the overlap. The tape is stitched to the underlap.

Step 1. To prepare the overlap side (on the left in the photo), I fused lightweight fusible along the edge of its extension to keep the fabric from raveling and to eliminate the need for any additional edge finishing. I'll be able to trim this edge to match the topstitching later, without affecting this finish. For the underlap, I cut a lining plenty wide enough to fold under itself when it gets topstitched closed later. I also extended the lining at the bottom to form a crotch-seam reinforcement. I stitched the lining to the underlap with a scant 1/4-inch (6 mm) seam allowance, right sides together, along the raw edge of the extension, from the waist at the top almost to the end of the curve at the bottom. Then, I trimmed the allowances at the curve, turned, and pressed.

Step 2. After folding the lining out of the way, I stitched the front crotch seam, starting about 1 inch (2.5 cm) from the inseam and stopping at the zipper X. There, I switched to a basting-stitch length before continuing up to the waist. Then I opened the pants, pressed a crease along the basted section, and laid them flat, face down.

Step 3. One of the main issues when sewing down the zipper at this stage is to keep the folded-under part of the tape narrow enough to be out of the way of the zipper teeth when the zipper's opened or closed. Also, you want to position the zipper itself well, but not too far, inside the fly opening. Using the basted opening seam as a guide, I positioned the zipper face down over it, with the teeth aligned to, and entirely on, the overlap side of the seam. Note that I folded the top of the

zipper tape over and slightly away from the slider so it's secured when stitched. I pinned the zipper in place, opening out the fly-shield lining so it remained free of the pins. Then, using a zipper foot, and trying to keep to the center of the tape and not too close to the teeth, I stitched the zipper tape to the shield once, not catching the shield lining underneath. Photo 3a shows the zipper folded over this stitching—a little wobbly, but certainly workable!

Step 4. Flipping the zipper back onto the overlap side, I could now stitch the free zipper tape to the fly facing (folding the pants front out of the way, of course). I used two rows of stitches instead of the single row I'd used on the other side. Notice that I folded under the top of the zipper tape on this side, too, before stitching, to finish it cleanly here.

3a. The zipper is folded over onto the underlap.

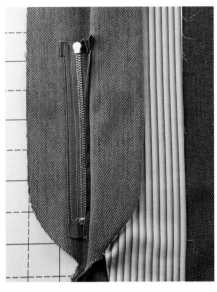

4. The zipper tape is stitched to the overlap with two rows of stitching.

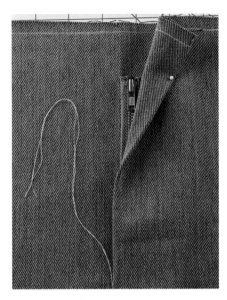

5. The basting is removed, and the waist-edge is marked.

Step 5. Next, I removed the basting stitches at the opening; and, with a few quick strokes of a chalk wheel across the fly, I established a consistent line for the top of the band finish on both sides, as shown in the photo. With a cut-on waistband, it's necessary to incorporate the waist finish into the zipper steps. I did not interface the band area on this sample (and might not on a garment made from this fabric), but a strip of lightweight fusible at the chalk line would create a useful edge to fold against and would provide an indelible stitching guide. Folding the overlap side right sides together at its top-edge clip, I transferred the marking to the overlap extension's wrong side, as shown in photo 5a.

Step 6. To prepare the underlap side, I finished forming the shield lining by folding under and pressing its long raw edge. Then, I folded the lined extension back over the pants front, with right sides together, as for the overlap side (photo 7).

5a. The overlap is folded right sides together. The waist-edge marking has been transferred to the wrong side.

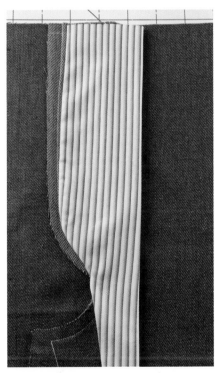

6. The underlap lining is folded under, along its long straight side.

7. The underlap and overlap waists are stitched. The petersham has been added.

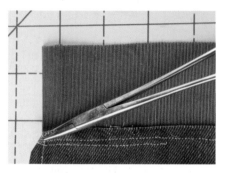

8. A hemostat helps you turn the overlap waist.

9. The overlap is basted and marked for topstitching (left). Then it's stitched and tacked (right).

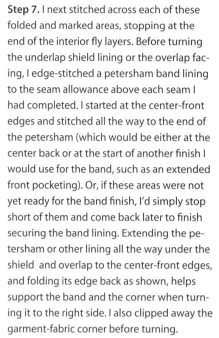

To illustrate the undesirable results of stitching stretched fabric, this sample shows a bias diagonal stitching line stretched at various angles to the line during stitching, which can result either in puckers or no puckers.

Step 7. I next stitched across each of these folded and marked areas, stopping at the end of the interior fly layers. Before turning the underlap shield lining or the overlap facing, I edge-stitched a petersham band lining to the seam allowance above each seam I had completed. I started at the center-front edges and stitched all the way to the end of the petersham (which would be either at the center back or at the start of another finish I would use for the band, such as an extended front pocketing). Or, if these areas were not yet ready for the band finish, I'd simply stop short of them and come back later to finish securing the band lining. Extending the petersham or other lining all the way under the shield and overlap to the center-front edges, and folding its edge back as shown, helps support the band and the corner when turning it to the right side. I also clipped away the garment-fabric corner before turning.

Step 8. To turn the corners right side out, I used my beloved hemostat to grasp the seam allowances precisely at the tip of the corner, as shown in the photo. Because this tool clamps shut to hold the clipped allowances, I can easily turn the corner around the tool and then use it to push out the corner fully without crumpling or distorting the allowances inside.

Step 9. After finishing and turning both the over- and underlapping sides of the closure, I topstitched both sides. The overlap topstitching, shown chalk-marked in photo 9, left, secures the front to the fly facing and keeps the zipper concealed. Sometimes I mark the entire line, but here I marked just the straight portion of the topstitching because I get smoother curves below that by concentrating on smooth hand movements and steady speed rather than by following a line. All I really need is a starting point (the end of the marked line) and an end point on the seam. The basting stitches hold the extension in place underneath. Their bottom position indicates where I should stitch to ensure I stay on the zipper tape—and also the line I need to stay close to, to avoid hitting the zipper teeth. Here I deliberately allowed the fabric to stretch across my stitching path as I stitched the bias portion of the seam, which created the slight puckers you can see in the photo at center. Avoid this!

Step 10. The underlap topstitching was simple. I just stitched a second line of stitches on the underlap zipper tape, from the right side. I caught the shield lining underneath at the same time and stitched as far down as I comfortably could at the bottom of the fly opening. Because I'd previously folded the lining's raw edge far enough under to extend beyond the zipper, this topstitching caught the folded-under edge to finish the lining.

Step 11. At the bottom of the shield facing, I made a short line of stitches catching the shield to the fly facing at the bottom of the curve, which keeps the zipper permanently covered from the inside. I also made a bar tack through all layers.

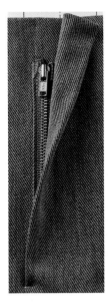

10. The underlap is topstitched and the shield lining secured, all in one.

11. The shield layers are joined to the overlap facing at the bottom of the curve. The fly is tacked through all layers.

12. The shield lining forms a tab to cover the crotch seam. The overlap facing is trimmed to match the shield.

Step 12. To form a tab from the extra fabric I allowed at the bottom of the shield lining when cutting it out, I pressed under its edges and tip, then hand-sewed it to cover the front crotch-seam allowances. I also I trimmed the edge of the overlap facing below the waist lining to follow the shape of the topstitching. Because this edge is fused underneath, it doesn't need any additional edge finishing.

In the photo at right, I've draped the zipper assembly over my sleeve board so you can see that the zipper-teeth ridge is only barely visible through a double layer of this denimlike fabric.

Okay, let's look at a somewhat more traditional zipper application, to see more options and to compare the results.

This medium-weight fabric nicely resists zipper-teeth imprinting.

TOPSTITCHING ZIPPERS

Stitching across the zipper teeth when topstitching the overlap inevitably creates wrinkles or bumps in the fly front at the base of the topstitching—an effect aggravated by very thin fabric. Many ready-to-wear manufacturers and some sewing teachers apparently think these bumps are no big deal (look at catalog shots for men's pants for examples). Some custom tailors and manufacturers disagree about the tape or will go so far as to remove metal zipper-teeth from cloth tapes below the stop before they catch the zipper tape, as on the Oxxford pants shown in the photo below. The easiest, and most reliable, way to keep the fabric completely smooth around the stitching is simply to fold the zipper tapes out of the way when topstitching.

You can remove zipper teeth to avoid hitting them when topstitching the fly.

ZIPPER FLY WITH AN ADD-ON SHIELD

This example shows a zipper for a garment that will have a separate waistband added after the zipper is complete (see page 99). This zipper is made with strategy A, shown in the drawing on page 79.

Step 1. Here, I'm attaching a separate shield, but will still start with a cut-on underlap extension. As with the cut-on waist zipper, I start by cutting both sides with facing/shield shapes so they curve down to about 1 inch (2.5 cm) below the point where I want to place the zipper stop, as shown in the photo. I put the excess zipper length at the top, where the trimmed ends will be covered by the band.

Step 2. I stitch the crotch seam to the zipper-end mark, then baste up the straight opening all the way to the top, pressing this seam open to separate the extensions.

Step 3. Then I place the zipper face down over this seam, with the teeth butting up to the ridge of the pressed-open seam, rather than sitting directly on the overlap facing as they were for the cut-on-waist zipper. (I want to stitch closer to the teeth in this method.)

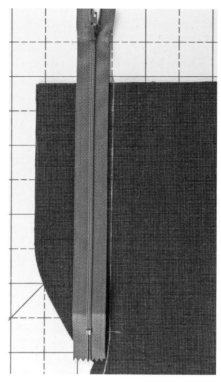

1. Here's the fly with an add-on band and shield, ready to go.

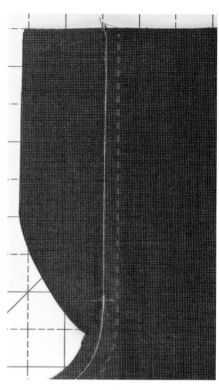

2. The crotch curve is stitched, and the center-front opening is basted.

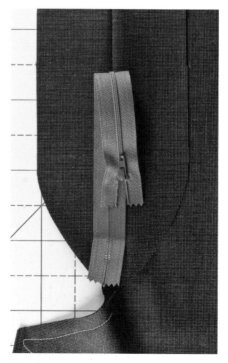

3. The zipper is positioned with the teeth over the seam.

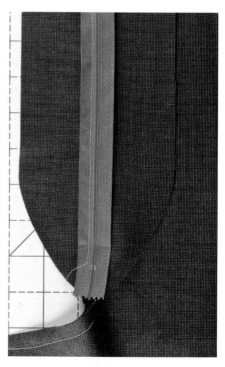

3a. The zipper tape is stitched close to the teeth.

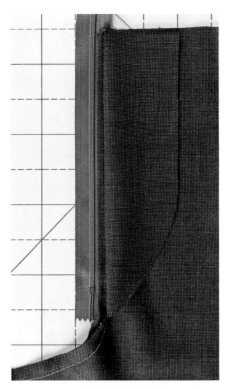

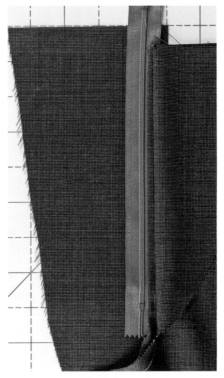

Step 4. Holding the zipper there, I stitch the tape to the shield extension, with a single row of stitches and using my zipper foot. I stitch closer to the teeth than to the edge of the tape, then press the zipper over so it's face up.

Step 5. Under the zipper, I place the straight, on-grain edge of a piece of fabric that is bigger than the shield I plan to cut, so that the inner edge extends about ¼ inch (6.4 mm) beyond the zipper tape.

Step 6. I trim the fabric piece to create the new shield, curving it so it extends below the zipper tape and is a little wider than the cut-on facing. Then I stitch the zipper tape close to the underlap fold to secure the shield (**6a**).

4. The zipper is pressed into finished position.

5. A new shield piece is positioned under zipper and underlap.

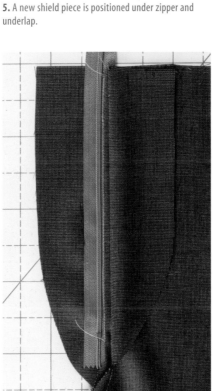

6. The new shield is trimmed to final shape.

6a. The new shield has been stitched in place.

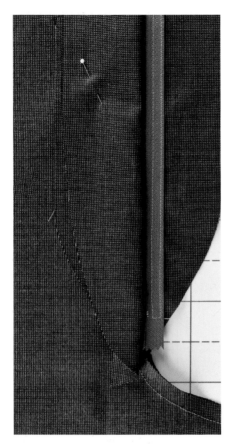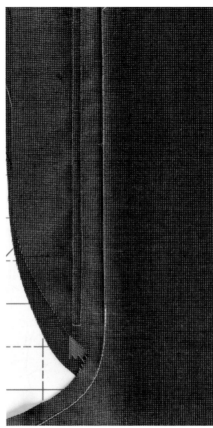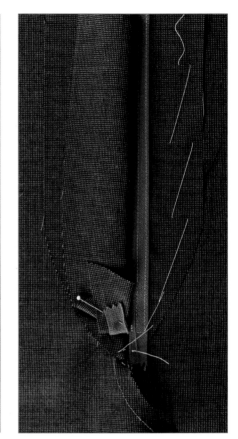

7. The opposite tape is secured to the overlap with two rows of stitching.

7a. Here's the overlap facing from the other side.

8. Here's the overlap facing basted in position, with the shield and left zipper tape folded out of the way.

Step 7. I turn the zipper assembly over and, folding the new shield layer out of the way, secure the free tape to the facing with a double row of stitches, turning at the zipper stop, as shown in photos 7 and 7a.

Step 8. To prepare for the topstitching that secures the facing, I baste the facing to the front, catching the zipper tape on the facing side, but not the other tape end (I don't want to add any unnecessary layers to the topstitching). I also catch the folded edge of the cut-on shield, but not the sewn-on one. In the photo, notice that the crotch-seam allowances are still together and are pressed

toward the zipper and that the basting is below the zipper stop. In the previous example, I had to open these seam allowances all the way to make sure not to catch the shield extension from the underlap side in this step. In that case, catching a fold here would interfere with its lying flat in its finished position; in this case, the folded shield is already in its finished position.

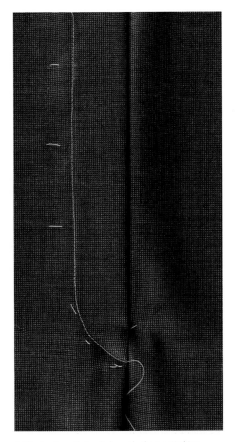

9. The basting stitches help guide the topstitching.

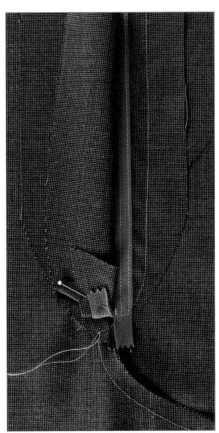

9a. The topstitching catches the crotch seam allowances.

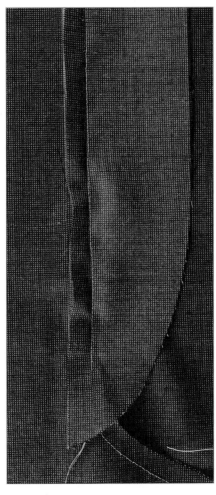

10. Trim away the shield extension below the straight edge of the attached shield.

Step 9. This time, I chalk-mark the topstitching line on the front. Then I topstitch between the basting stitches and the marked line, so I miss the zipper stop. I end (or start) exactly at the front crotch seam and catch the cut-on shield's folded edge on the inside, as shown in photo 9a. I could clip the crotch-seam allowances below the folded edge if I wanted to press the crotch seam open below the zipper, although I did not do that in the samples shown here.

Step 10. I remove the basting on the facing and at the zipper opening. Then I dust off the chalk and trim away the shield extension so it no longer extends beyond the sewn-on shield on the left. Finally, I bar-tack the opening through all layers.

COMPARING FINISHED ZIPPERS

Okay, let's look at a few ways in which different zipper constructions create subtle but visible distinctions. These details are the kinds of things that I enjoy tinkering with, but I won't be offended if you decide that my nitpicking goes off the charts here.

The add-on shield sample on pages 84–87 is the one with tan stitching shown in the photos here. Another sample is shown with blue stitching. Notice how the zipper teeth imprint through the overlap with blue stitching, even though this sample was fully interfaced. Its zipper tape was folded in half, as in the type-B sample with the cut-on shield, shown on pages 79–83. That construction method, although it produced a flat result, isn't necessarily the best choice on a thin fabric like this. The most raised portion of a type-A zipper, under the fly front, is the underlap fold. On a type-B zipper, it's the zipper teeth.

After a little gentle pressing, the imprinting temporarily disappears on the blue-stitched sample (C). You can see how much more smoothly the fabric lies around the blue topstitching at the base of the fly, compared to the tan-stitched fly, which dimples along the stitching because of the multiple layers caught underneath it. Also note the raised edge

Type-B zippers (left) can create a visible imprint through a thin fabric. **Type-A zippers** (right) are better in this case.

A and B: These crotch seam allowances are pressed toward the overlap and caught in the overlap topstitching.

C and D: These seam allowances are pressed open and not caught in the topstitching.

of the tan-stitched fly seam between the bar tack and the end of the topstitching, a permanent effect because the seam allowances here were all stitched toward the overlap

The seam allowances on the blue side weren't caught. Because they were initially clipped all the way to the zipper-stop dot, this seam could be pressed open all the way to the bar tack. You can see this pressed-open vs. pressed-to-the-side effect more clearly in the brown garment in the photos—the raised zipper teeth of an unfolded shield extension (photo **D**) and the raised front edge of a sewn-on shield (photo **B**). In sample D, I caught

the folded zipper tape in the topstitching, hence the lumps just below the stitching. Subtle effects, all, to be sure. Too subtle to matter? You decide.

Finally, in this last example, at right, notice that I bound the edges of the sewn-on shield for the ultimate in thinness: a single layer. Had I thought of it, I would have bound the edges before stitching the shield on in the first place, but it's nice to know that this can be done as an afterthought, too. Next time, I'll use a presser foot designed to help guide the binding (I ordered one right after making this sample).

A bound-edge, single-layer shield is about as thin an add-on shield as you can make.

Binding Edges

I'm usually quite content to leave interior raw edges very lightly finished, either with a simple zigzag stitch or some slightly more dense machine-overcasting stitch—or, if the edge has been fused, just leaving well enough alone. If you want a more polished look anywhere, such as on the fly, I suggest you use purchased rayon seam binding. It's ultra-thin and can be coaxed around corners even though it's not bias cut. If you want a binding fabric that matches your pocketing, for example, you could also make your own bias binding with one of those widely available binding-making gizmos, such as the Clover brand shown in the photo at far right.

BUTTON FLIES

Okay, you may not want a button fly on your pants—but, just in case, I'm going to show you how it's done. I like button flies. The technique is actually pretty interesting and does have applications beyond pant flies. You might want to adapt it to a coat or a jacket front, for example, as a concealed-button closure.

Integrating the fly into a cut-on waist finish is what makes this technique so interesting: How to finish the top of the fly if there's no band to simply bind over it? The answer is an old favorite of mine, last seen at the top of the slant pocket: the clipped seam, which does one thing on one side of the clip and another on the other side. In the photo at bottom left, the seams at the front edge of the fly overlap join to form a single layer in the band area; but about 2 inches (5.1 cm) from the top edge, they're clipped to form the two layers of a covered buttonhole strip.

This buttonhole strip is what makes the button fly different from the zipper fly. Otherwise, the parts are the same. There's a faced shield extending from the center front on the fly underlap, here called the button strip. The fly overlap has a facing, folded back from the center front edge. The buttonhole strip is layered in between.

All three parts are faced with a lightweight fabric to reduce bulk—or with self (garment) fabric if it's lightweight. As you can see, I take this opportunity to unleash my patchwork heart, but you can be as restrained here as you like, with self-fabric facing the world and pocketing only on the inside. The pattern pieces you'll need are shown at bottom right and on the facing page.

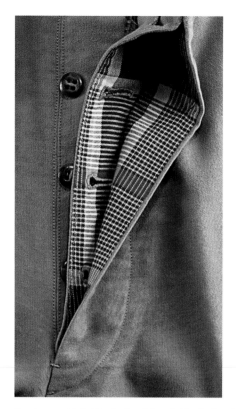 

There's no need to hold back when lining a button fly. Experiment with fabric choices.

A cut-on band can be easily integrated into a button-fly front.

BUTTON-FLY PATTERN

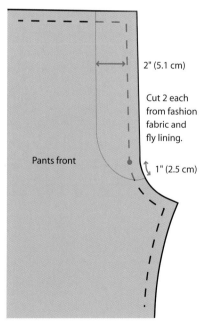

2" (5.1 cm)

Cut 2 each from fashion fabric and fly lining.

Pants front

1" (2.5 cm)

Trace your button-fly pattern from your front piece, without fly outlets or cut-on extensions.

BUTTON-FLY PARTS

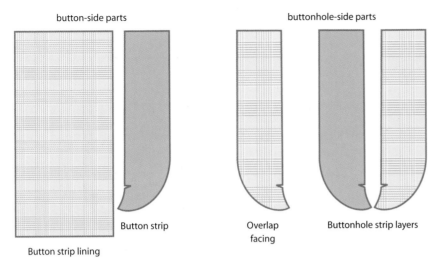

button-side parts

Button strip lining

Button strip

buttonhole-side parts

Overlap facing

Buttonhole strip layers

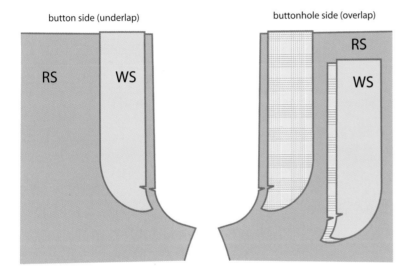

button side (underlap)

RS   WS

buttonhole side (overlap)

RS

WS

Cut four pieces from the fly pattern, two each from lining and garment fabrics, each pair mirrored (or two mirrored pairs from lightweight garment fabric only). Also cut a rectangle of lining twice as wide and a little longer than the fly pieces.

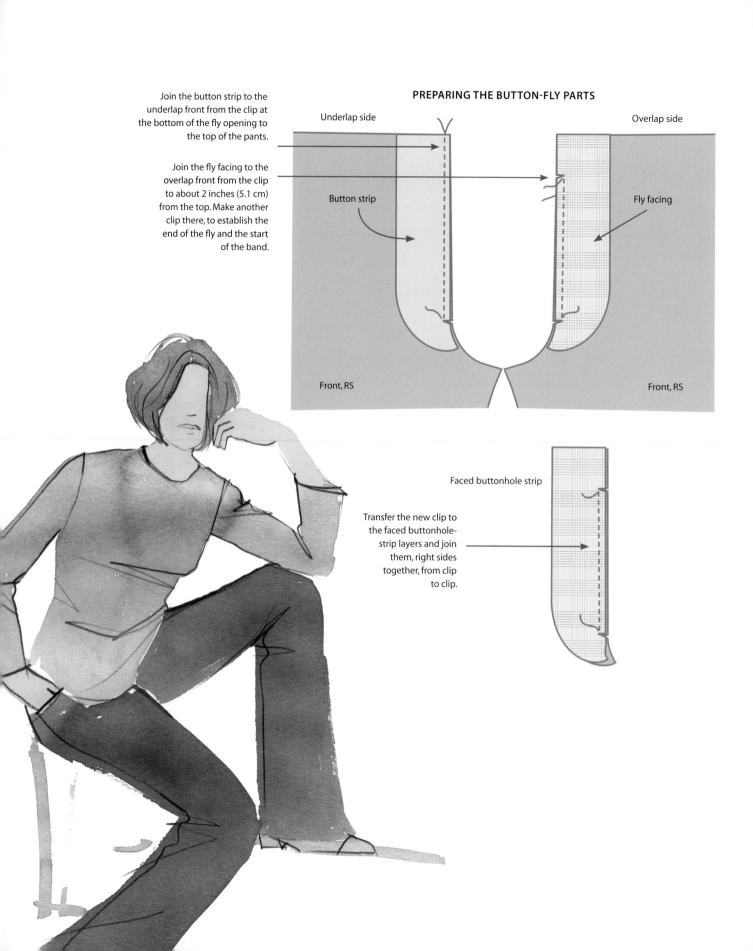

PREPARING THE BUTTON-FLY PARTS

Join the button strip to the underlap front from the clip at the bottom of the fly opening to the top of the pants.

Join the fly facing to the overlap front from the clip to about 2 inches (5.1 cm) from the top. Make another clip there, to establish the end of the fly and the start of the band.

Underlap side

Overlap side

Button strip

Fly facing

Front, RS

Front, RS

Faced buttonhole strip

Transfer the new clip to the faced buttonhole-strip layers and join them, right sides together, from clip to clip.

Here's the buttonhole strip, faced with a complementary fabric.

The strip is turned right side out. The red markings indicate the suggested hole placement.

After the strip assembly is joined to the overlap at the band/front, trim the seam at the corner.

You can decide to arrange the lining layer inside or outside of the buttonhole strip, depending on what you want to see on the inside of the finished pants. You can decide this after you cut, too, because all the parts are mirrored pairs. I usually place the lining layer inside the strip so I can enjoy the lining fabric when I button the fly, which is what I've done with these samples in the photos. If you want the lining positioned the other way, just put it underneath the strip before stitching.

Turn and press the facing of the overlap side. Turn and press the buttonhole strip's facing to the inside, as shown in the center photo. Now you'll make your buttonholes. In my experience, four is plenty; three would do fine, too, if the opening is not too long.

Place the turned buttonhole strip, right sides together, under the faced overlap front. Stitch all the layers together around the center-front corner, from the upper clip to the end of the facings along the top. I usually choose to stitch a curve at the corner, as shown in the photo at far right, but that's optional. Trim the seam allowances at the corner and turn the strip to the inside.

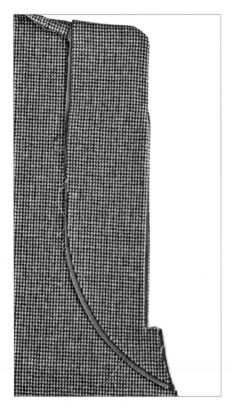

After trimming the seam allowances, turn the button-hole strip to the inside.

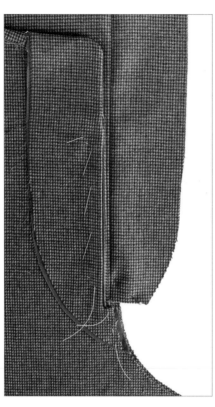

Offset the edges of the fly layers and baste them in position.

The crotch seam is basted to hold the two layers in position. Here, the basted seam is folded open, revealing the layers below.

LINING THE BUTTON STRIP

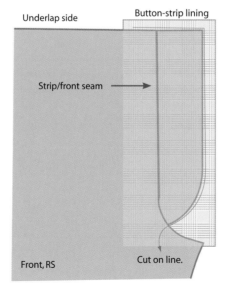

Underlap side   Button-strip lining

Strip/front seam →

Front, RS   Cut on line.

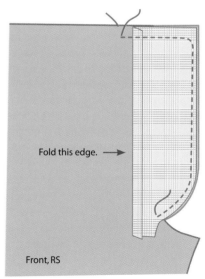

Fold this edge. →

Front, RS

Cut the underlap/button-strip lining after
joining the strip to the front.

Now, as you join the two fronts, you can line up the front crotch seams and baste the layers to arrange the offset of the various edges precisely to keep the inner layers fully concealed under the overlap layer, as shown in the center photo on the facing page. Note how I've arranged the buttonhole strip's edge just short of the front edge, basted to hold it there (catching only that layer), then offset the whole overlap side a little to the left of the button-strip seam on the underlap layer at the bottom.

I basted the crotch seam to hold the two layers in that position, as you can see when the basted seam is opened and it's all turned over, as in the photo at far right on the facing page—showing how all will fall when the crotch seam is stitched. Also note that the button strip has not been caught in any of the basting and won't be caught in the sewn crotch seam.

I could equally well wait until all the steps are completed before joining the two sides at the crotch—this flexibility is part of why I like making these button closures. Everything stays discrete for as long as possible, and there are plenty of opportunities to tweak the positioning and finish of all the parts.

The next step is to line the button strip. Lay the strip/front assembly over your lining fabric and trace around it to cut the lining needed. Then arrange this piece, right sides together, over the strip to stitch it, as shown in the drawing on the facing page. If you haven't cut the lining with a selvage at its inner edge, fold that edge over before stitching, making sure that the fold and the fold allowance extend past the strip/front seam, so both will be caught when you topstitch the strip/front seam to secure the lining. You're forming the top edge of the cut-on waist-band with this stitching, so match the right and left top-edge seam lines carefully before you proceed. If you plan on inserting a hook and eye, you should do that first. If you're finishing the band with petersham, turn the buttonhole-strip/front seam inside out again. Attach the petersham to the top-edge seam allowances—the underlap side, too—before you turn the button-strip lining right side out.

The final step, before adding the buttons, is to topstitch both sides through all layers on the overlap side to form the visible fly topstitching and secure the buttonhole strip. Also topstitch on the underlap side, to catch the strip facing underneath, either in the ditch of the strip/front seam or right next to it. (I usually stitch once on each side.) The buttonhole-strip basting you stitched previously will hold those layers securely in place as you topstitch through them.

The photo at right, of a button fly during construction, shows how the front crotch seam doesn't have to catch the end of the buttonhole strip at all because the strip is held by the topstitching. In this case, because I added an extension (1) to the button strip to reinforce the crotch seam (2), I decided the finished effect would be too bulky if I also included the end of the buttonhole strip/facing in that seam. The strip/facing will sit nicely under the reinforcement, but needn't be secured there. Note how the raw edges of this buttonhole strip assembly are simply finished with machine overcasting (3).

There are buttons specifically designed for button flies. They have little grooves between the thread holes so the threads can lie below the surface of the button. They are also rimless, so the whole button is as flat and smooth as possible. Ask or search for 22L trouser-fly bottons at any tailoring supply source or check the sources on page 132. Similar buttons, slightly larger, are available for suspenders.

TOPSTITCHING THE BUTTON FLY

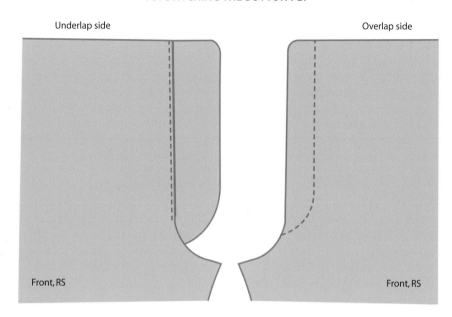

Underlap side

Overlap side

Front, RS

Front, RS

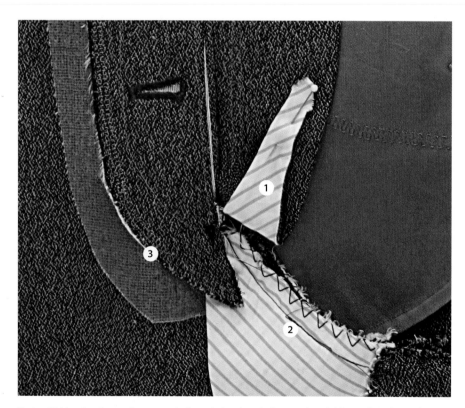

The topstitching alone is enough to secure the buttonhole strip, so its lower end needn't be caught in the crotch seam.

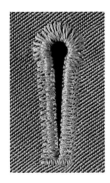

This eyelet-based keyhole buttonhole was stitched twice at different widths.

KEYHOLE BUTTONHOLES

Keyhole buttonholes are designed to prevent distortion when the closure is under strain during wear. These buttonholes—shaped like a partial eyelet with legs—allow the garment to stay flat around your buttons when buttoned, whether the shank is integral to the button or is created by the attaching thread. Without the extra space provided by the keyhole shape, an ordinary buttonhole will be distorted as the shank pulls against the end of the hole. On pants, I'd suggest using keyholes for any and all buttonholes, whether on button flies, pocket flaps, or waist closures.

I only recently got a sewing machine that could make keyhole buttonholes, but I had already developed a way of making keyhole buttonholes with an eyelet plate. I like the results so well that I still prefer to make them this way on my new machine. Eyelet-based holes are stitched after the hole at the end is cut, so the stitches both cover the raw edge and radiate around the hole (unlike those I'd get using my keyhole presets). You'll find the tools and step-by-step process I use to make these buttonholes on the companion DVD-ROM. Don't proceed without making a few practice buttonholes on your pants fabric with any inner- or under-layers you intend to have in the finished garment.

CHAPTER SIX

WAISTBANDS

No matter how you've designed (or chosen) your waistband area to look on the outside, it needs to provide strength, stability, and security. The techniques and strategies herein aim to do all that as unobtrusively and as easily as possible. If you plan to supplement your waistbands with a belt, you'll find all the information you need to make and attach a wide variety of belt loops here, too.

SEW-ON WAISTBAND

My technique for adding a waistband to a pair of pants picks up where my second zipper-insertion discussion left off—with the zipper finished in front and only the zipper tape extending above the pants (pages 84–87). It makes sense that the front pockets should be finished before you begin, and you'd most likely want to have the side seams and back pockets completed, too.

Step 1. My waistbands are always divided at center back and faced, not folded. I interface the bands with rectangles of fusible interfacing that extend only to the seam lines, not into the seam allowances. The interfacing is there as much to create an edge to fold against and a stitching guide for attaching them, as to provide firmness (of which I

don't need much). The bands should be long enough to extend beyond each front by the width of the fly shield/facing, plus a ¼-inch (6.4 mm) seam allowance.

Step 2. Sew the underlap side of the band first, so you can more easily shape the overlap to cover it. Press the band's front-edge seam allowance to the wrong side; then stitch the bands to the pants, as shown in the area marked with red, stopping at the pant's edge. Trim the zipper tapes after stitching the bands over them, as shown in the photo. I like to remove more teeth than tape because the teeth are stiffer than the tape and are more likely to be felt by the wearer; the tape, on the other hand, is necessary to keep the zipper positioned securely in the seam.

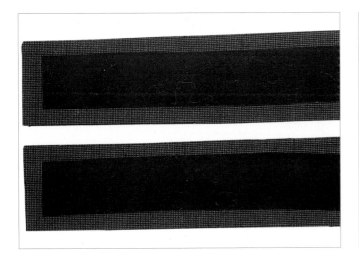

1. The waistband pieces are interfaced to the seam lines for easy folding and stitching.

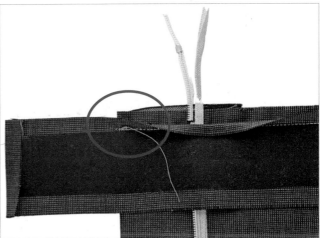

2. An underlap band is joined across a zipper fly, with the excess zipper trimmed.

3. The underlap band is turned up and back against itself. A petersham lining is stitched to its top edge.

4. The band and lining are turned to the inside. The arrow indicates where to press allowances above the fly. The circle shows the clipping that allows the opening of the seam beyond the fly.

Step 3. Fold up the bands and fold their extensions back over them. Cut lengths of petersham that can be folded over at their front edges and still extend to cover the band as far back as you need them to, depending on your preferred waist finish (pages 108–109). Position the petersham on the right side of the band, to cover only the upper-band seam allowance, glue-basting it in place with fusible tape if you like. Then edge-stitch the petersham all the way to its opposite end—or at least for a few inches (centimeters) beyond the fly.

Step 4. Turn the band over the pants, tucking the inside band/pants seam allowances up into the band.

Step 5. You can clip the band/pants seam allowances anywhere beyond the vertical zipper/fly seam lines, which will allow you to press the allowances open to create a flat transition from the pants to the band from there on out (obviously, your petersham needs to be wide enough to cover the open seam completely, as shown in the photo).

5. The petersham covers the opened seam (it's not yet finished above the fly).

Now you're ready to insert the hook-and-eye closure. Hooks and eyes come in two common varieties for pants: sew-on (below top) and clamp-on (below bottom). You're likely used to seeing the clamp-on type on ready-to-wear pants. This type is definitely my first choice for a hook set, even though it's less commonly available to home sewers. You'll need a pair of needle-nose pliers to insert the hook and eye. Bent-tip ones are especially handy, as you'll see. A clamp-on hook and eye is attached while the band is still open inside. If you'd prefer to use the sew-on type, you can attach the hook and eye after the band is finished.

Attach sew-on hooks and eyes (top) after the band is finished. Attach clamp-on hooks (bottom) and eyes while the band is being finished.

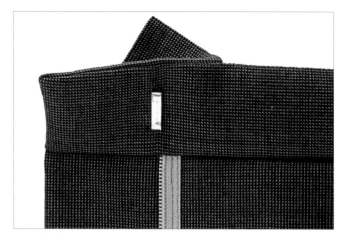

6. Position the clamp-on eye above the underlap zipper teeth.

6a. Needle-nose pliers help you bend down the eye's prongs.

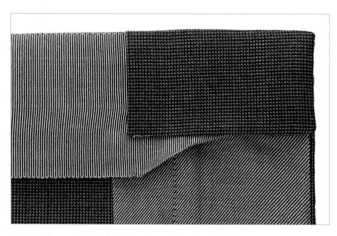

7. Fold the petersham under the band extension above the fly.

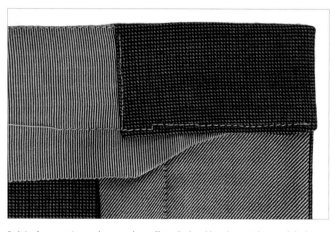

8. Join the extension to the petersham. Close the band by edge-stitching and ditch-stitching from the front.

9. Align the overlap band to the underlap at the band/garment seam.

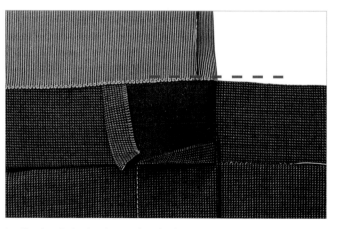

9a. Also align the band at the petersham/band seam.

Step 6. For clamp-ons, position the eye first, directly above the zipper teeth, as shown in photo 6. Push its prongs through the fabric layers, catching the petersham, but not the inside band fabric. Place the backing plate over the prongs, with the depression in the plate pointing downward against the petersham. Bend the prongs over it, as shown in photo 6a.

Step 7. Fold both the petersham's lower edge and the band extension's lower seam allowance up into the band, within the area of the extension. The petersham will be folded at an angle, so it can lie flat as it extends around the pants, covering the opened seam below it, as shown in the photo. You can either let it unfold before the end of the band extension, as I need to do here to cover the clipped seams, or after the extension if the clip is farther away from the fly.

Step 8. Finally, join the extension to the petersham only. Then edge-stitch from the front along the bottom of the band, catching all layers. I stitch just above the ditch of the seam until just beyond the zipper, to ensure that I catch the folded-up edge underneath. Then I jog down to the ditch before proceeding to catch the petersham, which is now hanging straight down.

Step 9. The band on the overlap side is created exactly the same way. Take care to align both the band/garment seam lines, as shown in photo 9, and the petersham/band seam line, across the center-front opening, as shown in photo 9a.

10. The overlap band/garment seam allowances are clipped at an angle for easier coverage by the folded petersham.

10a. The petersham can fold within the extension if the seam-clip is moved away from the front.

Step 10. On the overlap side, I clip the band/garment seam allowances at an angle and farther from the front, as shown in photos 10 and 10a. This way, I have room to let the petersham flatten out only after coming out of the end of the band extension (probably the more attractive option, at least on the inside, compared to how I handled this on the other side (shown in photo 7 on page 102).

To complete installation of the hook and eye, position the hook by slipping it onto the attached eye. Then zip the pants closed. When the turned overlap band looks properly aligned, pinch down on the hook's prongs and push them through the band and the petersham layers. Pull the hook off the eye and then secure it to the backing plate, as you did the eye. If you inadvertently flatten the hook while trying to fold over the prongs, pry it back open again with the blade of a flat screwdriver. (See the video clips on the companion DVD-ROM for a second option.)

Step 11. Topstitch the band in the ditch of the band/garment seam line to catch the inner band and petersham, as shown in the photo. You'll barely see the thread if the thread color matches the garment fabric.

11. Topstitch the bands in the ditch of the band/garment seam, and the thread is virtually invisible.

EXTENDED WAISTBAND

So, let's say you want an extended band. Here's how I'd do it:

Step 1. When you cut the extended band, add twice the finished extension's length. Then stitch the band to the garment, stopping at the front edge, as you did for the sew-on waistband (page 99, step 2).

Step 2. Then press the band up and fold the extension back over itself. Press under the short edge. Press up the band's lower seam allowances all the way to the end of the waistband.

Step 3. If you want a petersham-band finish, lay the petersham over the upper-band seam allowances on the band's right side, just as I described for the band without an extension (page 100). Stitch the petersham to the band along the band's upper seam allowance.

Suppose you're fresh out of petersham? Or you simply prefer to use a lining fabric or pocketing? Working with fabric is a perfectly acceptable option, but you'll still want to cut the fabric long enough to fill the entire band extension, in order to provide support for the clamp-on hook and eye that comes later, as shown on page 106.

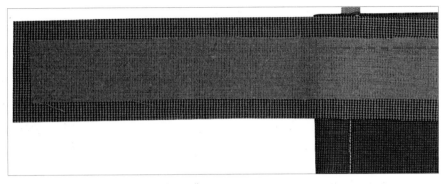

1. Prepare and stitch an extended-tab band just like a band that is not extended, but make it longer.

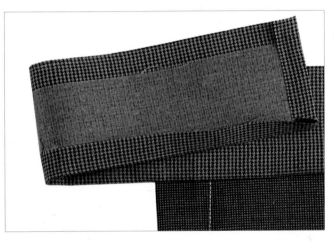

2. Press up the band and band/garment seam allowances, then fold the band over itself, right sides together.

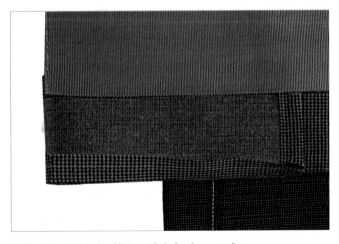

3. Align the petersham band lining with the band-top seam line.

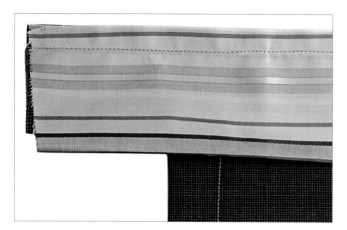

4. Stitch a double-fold of band-lining fabric, following the top edge of the band interfacing.

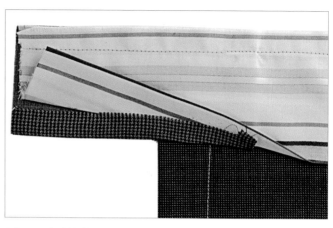

5. Press up the folded lower edges of the lining at an angle, within the band's lower seam-allowance fold.

Step 4. If you're using fabric, not petersham, cut the fabric so it's the length of the band and twice its finished width plus two seam allowances. Fold and press the fabric in half lengthwise, right sides out. On the right side of the pants, align the raw edges with the band's upper raw edges. Stitch the band lining, working on the wrong side so you can follow the upper edge of the interfacing.

Step 5. Before turning the band right side out, fold and press the lining up at an angle, so it fits inside the band extension and blends back to its original width shortly beyond the band edge. The folded lining also fills out the extension nicely.

Step 6. Clamp-on hooks are awkward to install, and an extension with a hook is a bear to turn right side out. I turn the extension with the band open at the bottom so I can easily get in there to install the hook without having to turn the band afterward. The lining, pressed to create a double layer, extends to the end of the band so it can get caught in the hook's prongs and also can provide support for the band, just as the petersham would.

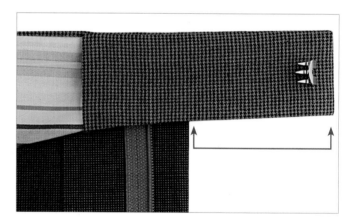

6. Install a clamp-on hook before hand-stitching the bottom edge of the band extension as indicated by the red line.

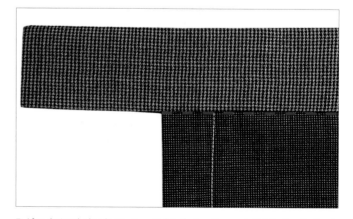

7. After closing the band extension, stitch in the band/garment ditch to close the band.

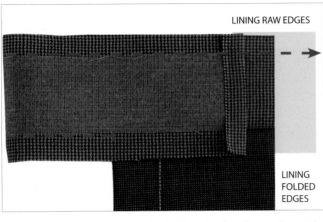

LINING RAW EDGES

LINING FOLDED EDGES

7a. If you don't want to add a clamp-on hook or do any hand stitching, machine-stitch as indicated by the red lines. The pink rectangle indicates the lining placement.

I insert the hook as described on page 102 (install the hook first, then line up the eye to match it on the opposite band). Then I close the bottom of the band as invisibly as possible, felling it by hand.

Step 7. When that's done, I return to machine sewing, stitching in the ditch of the band/pant seam from the edge of the pants, just as for a band without an extension.

If I preferred to sew on the hook from the outside and didn't mind turning the extension (kind of a pain even without a hook in the way), I could have simply stitched the extension as shown in photo 7a, starting the lining just inside the folded band edge (indicated by the tinted area). But I like those pronged hooks best; and I much prefer to shape the extension from the right side, pressing the edges and end until they look great—rather than stitching and turning it, and hoping it still looks good and lies flat after all that pulling and poking. Choices, yet again.

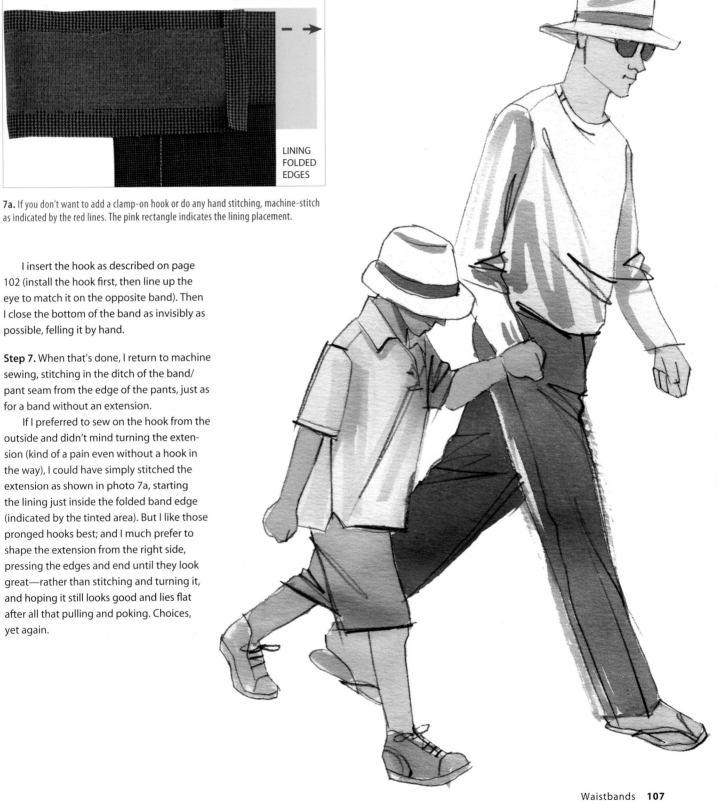

HOW MUCH PETERSHAM?

So, where should you use petersham (or other type of lining) to finish the waist-band? I see three reasonable options:

Option 1. Line all the way to the center back, in one piece, as shown in the top photo.

Option 2. Line to the front edge of the front pocket, which finishes the rest of the front; then line from the back of that pocket to the center back, in two pieces, as shown in the second photo.

Option 3. Line only the areas around the pockets from front to center back, letting the pockets finish the band above, in three pieces, as shown in the third photo.

The differences are simply a matter of preference or convenience. Option 1 is done entirely by machine and requires that you press some shape into the petersham to make its bottom edge longer, to accommodate the pant shape below the waist. Options 2 and 3 call for hand stitching at the top and edges of the pockets, because that's how they get secured to the top of the band (see page 19). The shorter petersham pieces don't need to be shaped, but they can be, with an iron, even after they're attached, if it helps them lie nicely. You decide.

Option 1: Line the entire band.

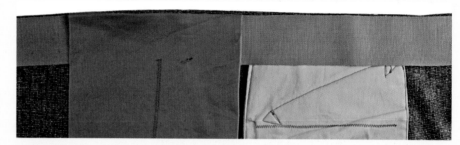
Option 2: Line the front to the pocket, then line the entire back.

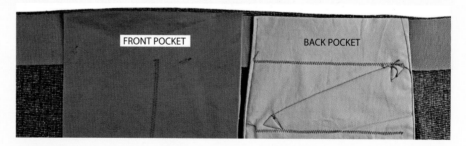

FRONT POCKET   BACK POCKET

Option 3: Line only the areas around the pockets from front to center back.

You can iron the petersham to shape it, either before or after attaching one side of it to the garment.

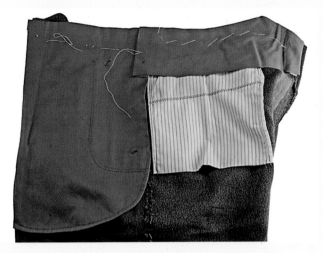

Here's another option: no petersham. Shape the band with pocketing fabric instead.

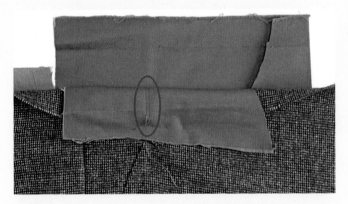

Because part of this pocket is caught in the pocket topstitching, it has to be clipped to fold with the garment edge.

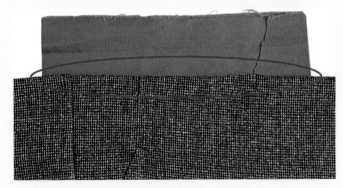

Form the pant-top edge first, then form the pocket-top edge to match.

Before I discovered petersham and abandoned waist stiffeners, I took a different approach. In front, the pockets took care of business, finished at the top with hand stitches. I'd fill any gaps with hand-inserted scraps, à la Stanley Hostek (page 22). In back, I liked a shaped band, so I'd machine-stitch some pocketing cut on-grain (so the bottom edge could be placed on the selvage) onto the back, as shown in the top photo. The belt loops held the front stiffener and back-pocket tops securely all around.

I'm still very fond of this front-pocket-as-band-finish idea, so that's what I did in the samples in the center and bottom photos at left. They have slant-front pockets, so I need to clip away the excess pocketing I stitched into when topstitching the front/facing seam. From here on out, it's just a matter of folding the upper band and pocketing edges under to make a smooth top, blending it into the petersham-finished front closure.

Loop strips cut on a selvage don't need to be turned, just topstitched.

A basic loop, not caught in any nearby seam, offers maximum placement flexibility.

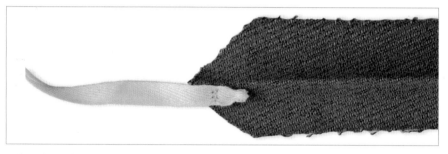

1. Shape the end of a loop strip before turning. Then attach a thin tape or strong string that is longer than the strip.

2. Enclose the tape when stitching the turned strip. Then press.

BELT-LOOP OPTIONS

The lowly belt loop definitely deserves your attention. It's almost as rich with design opportunities as a pocket and can almost always be added as an afterthought.

I prefer a turned loop that's not caught in the waistband seam and isn't folded over the top of the band, letting the belt slide all the way to the top edge of the pants. (Horrors!) Those loop-securing methods are what you'll find in most belt-loop instructions, and you're welcome to them, if you prefer. I attach my loops individually and set them down about 3/8 inch (1 cm) from the band edge.

Regardless of where you'd like to position your loops, the essential idea is that all of the loops styles and variations shown in this book can be, and ought to be, attached after everything else at the top of the pants is finished. They should be stitched on through all layers—so they also serve admirably to hold any waistband finishes in place. But first, let's be sure you can turn belt-loop strips easily. (Of course, if you don't mind topstitching your loops and have enough selvage available, you can skip turning them altogether, as shown in the photo at top left.)

TURNING A LOOP STRIP

Before making the final loops, do a practice run with your garment fabric. Cut an 18- by 1 1/2-inch (45.7 x 3.8 cm) on-grain test strip to see how belt-loop turning works and make some loops to play with. Press the strip lightly in half lengthwise, with right sides together. Then cut off one end at an angle. Triple-stitch a 20-inch (50.8 cm) length of linen tape or strong string to the wrong side near the fold (**1**). Lay the tape or string inside the fold. Then stitch the strip into a long tube with a 1/4-inch (6 mm) seam allowance and the tape inside it, taking care not to catch the tape in the stitching (**2**). Press the seam allowances open. Pull the tape through the tube to turn the belt-loop strip right-side-out. Center the seam line and press thoroughly.

POSITIONING AND STITCHING LOOPS

Typically, and minimally, pants have seven belt loops: one at each side seam, one at center back, and one in the middle of each waistband quadrant. In back, the loops are centered over each back pocket; in front, they're placed at each front pleat or dart, or centered between center front and the sides, as shown in the drawing below. The choice of any arrangement or quantity beyond these minimums is a designer's detail.

To stitch on a simple loop, I glue-stick my cut-to-length loop in place (**3**). Then I satin-stitch across the butted raw edges with a wide stitch setting (**4**). I chalk-mark the upper edge on which I want my loops to line up, then roll the loop open so I can straight-stitch across it at the line (**5**). You can do the same thing at the lower end, if you like, but gravity and your belt will naturally take care of that end.

3. Glue-stick to baste the loop.

4. Satin-stitch the ends together, with the loop held out of the way.

5. Roll the loop so you can secure the top with narrow satin or straight stitching.

LOOP PLACEMENT

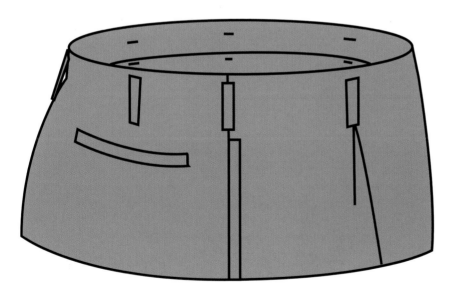

Place loops at each side seam and at center back, then equally spaced in between.

One end of this basic turned loop has been shaped into a triangular tip and topstitched.

The unshaped top of the turned loop is tacked on the inside.

SHAPED LOOPS

I usually prefer a shaped belt loop. A fabric-sculpture micro-experience, the shaped loop, shown at far left, is nothing but a turned tube that has been massaged with scissors, glue-stick, and an iron to form a tiny triangular tip. The tip gets topstitched in place instead of stitched from the inside, like its upper part-ner, the raw unshaped other end, shown in the photo at left.

The following steps will work to create more elaborate belt loops of almost any shape.

Step 1. Cut the desired shape from fusible interfacing. Fuse the interfacing to a scrap of pants fabric.

Fold the scrap's edges over and glue-baste them onto the shape within. You can unstick the glue and redo the shaping as needed until you're completely happy with the shape.

Step 2. Secure the shaped edges with a scrap of lightweight fusible. Topstitch, if desired, then secure.

1. Form this loop by pressing around a fusible, perma-nent template.

2. Secure the shaping with another piece of light fusible.

2a. Here's the completely shaped loop, from the right side. No turning involved.

BUTTONHOLE LOOPS

The buttonhole loop is the belt loop's cousin. Made from the same turned tube, it's cleverly folded to form a point, then inserted into pocket mouths and garment edges. This simple structure has seen centuries of use as a stitch-on buttonhole. The secret to its perfect formation is revealed here for the first time: Overlap the sides while bar-tacking it closed for a gapless finish, as shown in the photos at far right.

This simple folded tube has considerable potential as a dramatic, decorative belt loop. A few stitching options are shown in the center photo.

If you'd like to explore a V-shaped version, make a little cardboard template, such as the one in the photo below at right, to help you set the V angle identically for each loop. Secure it as described for the shaped loops, with a combination of topstitching and concealed satin stitches. (And send me a picture of your finished creation!)

A buttonhole loop is also made from a turned-tube strip, then folded.

Overlap the sides while topstitching the point, to reduce gapping.

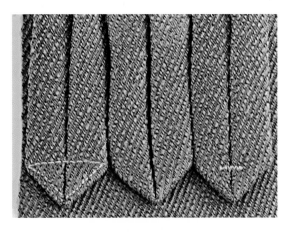

Here are three topstitching options: triangular stitching, hidden stitching, and simple tacking.

Spread the sides for a V-shaped loop. Use a template as shown at right to create a consistent spread on multiple loops.

CHAPTER SEVEN

REFINEMENTS

This chapter contains several tips and techniques that I've found very helpful as I've continued to refine my results as a trousers-maker, but they aren't essential to the process. Take hand stitches, for example. You can make great trousers without ever picking up a hand needle, but if you're willing to give the few hand stitches described here a whirl, you'll significantly expand the range of details you can explore. I've also included a few techniques here that I personally don't use, such as shaping pant legs and using ready-made band finishes, because you may find them helpful in your work. If you do, I hope you'll fill me in on what I'm missing!

LINING FLAPS

When you're lining a corner—as on a pocket flap, for example—you want the lining to be smaller than the outer layer, so you can press the turned edges and hide the lining underneath. First, I trim the lining about $1/8$ inch (3 mm) along all the edges that will be turned. On the flap, I fold each corner diagonally. Then I pin through the folded edge, just catching the fold a few times, as shown in the top photo below. I stop about $1/2$ inch (1.3 cm) from the seam edge, gathering a little fullness there. Next, I press around the pin to flatten the area a bit, making it a little easier to arrange against the lining. I hand-baste the layers at the seam line, matching the raw edges as closely as possible. Next, I machine-stitch all around. When I remove the pin the outer layer expands, and I'm ready to turn and press the corner.

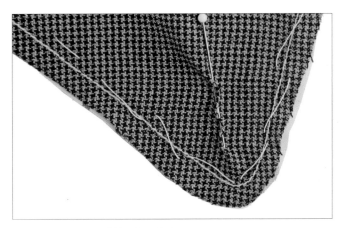

A pin inserted at a corner fold gathers a little ease

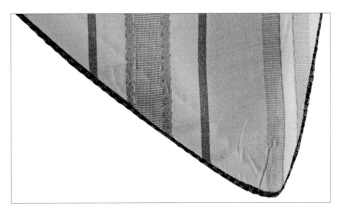

When released, the ease allows the lining to hide underneath after the corner is turned.

STITCHING THE CROTCH

 All of my methods for the fly result in the pants being joined in front only, before the leg seams are sewn (the button fly, page 90, can also be done with the legs as tubes, if desired). The rest of the crotch and center-back seam are sewn after joining the leg inseams and side seams. When you're joining the legs at the back crotch seam, it may prove handy to have one leg inside the other, with right sides together and a wrong side showing. So, before sewing, with right sides out, reach into the top of one leg and out through its hem. Then, grab both hems and pull them back together through the leg. It will now be relatively easy to access the entire center-back seam for stitching, as you can see in the photo below. (Note: The fusible strips on the center back seams in the photo are there to keep this quite loosely woven fabric from pulling at the seam, which, to my dismay, revealed itself as a problem during construction. They're not necessary in pants made of firmly woven, stable fabric).

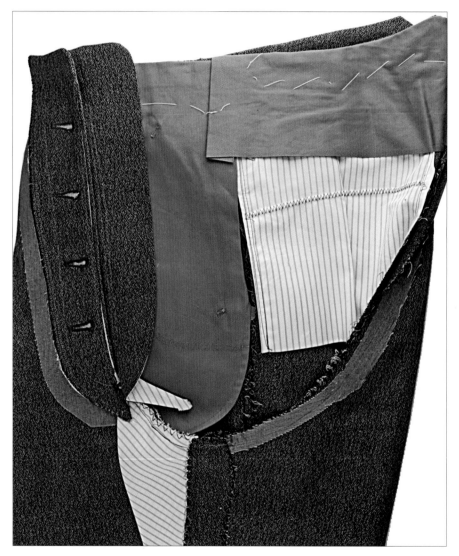

Placing one leg inside the other may simplify stitching the crotch and center back.

SHAPING THE LEGS

For old-time tailors, an essential part of the garment-making process was the skillful shaping of virtually every piece of flat wool in the garment. The tailor used an iron and steam to shrink and stretch different portions of the fabric, to provide contour and form beyond what could be achieved with seams alone. It's hard for us in the ready-to-wear age even to imagine the effectiveness of this once-common practice, but two things seem clear: First, not all the fabrics we might want to use for pants will shape equally well. Second, it takes a good deal of practice and experience to do this shaping properly without misshaping your precious garment in the process.

At right, there's a rendering of an illustration from one of my old tailoring books, by J. E. Liberty, that shows clearly what these craftsmen were up to when they shaped pant legs. It's particularly interesting to note that the author of this 1933 publication considered that "turn-up" trousers (those with cuffs) shouldn't be shaped the same as "plain," or uncuffed, ones. The basic idea is that you stretch first by pulling the fabric as you iron it. Then you shrink out the ripples that the stretching causes elsewhere in the garment by gradually forcing them into smaller half-circular areas at the garment edge—using lots of steam.

Stanley Hostek has an interesting take on the subject. When I first began to correspond with him, I asked him about this shaping business. As he explained it, you don't really even need an iron. All you need do is ease the fronts to the backs above the knee, and the backs to the fronts below the knee—by about 3/8 inch (10 mm) in each case—by stretching the shorter piece against the longer one as you sew the seams. I've tried this, of course; and I'm sorry to say I didn't notice any difference in either the comfort or drape of my pants, except when I overdid it and the end result looked terrible!

FOR THE TRADITIONALIST: A FULLY SHAPED LEG

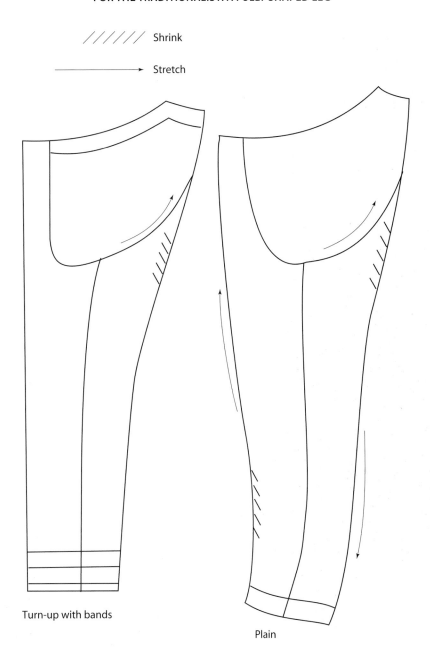

////// Shrink

———→ Stretch

Turn-up with bands

Plain

So, what's the upshot of all this? I retain two ideas from this noble tradition; neither is essential to a satisfying trouser, but both are easy to do and not risky:

Step 1. Stretch the entire center-back crotch seam while stitching it, primarily to protect the stitches there from breaking when worn. Most tailors also stitch this seam twice to strengthen it.

Step 2. Ease the front onto the back at the inseam from the knee to the crotch by stretching the back while stitching the inseam, as shown in the drawing below. Note that the rear inseam has been cut about ½ inch (1.3 cm) shorter than the front inseam in preparation for this step. I've sometimes left out this step; I never regretted it, or even noticed a difference. I still do it when I think of it, just in case it's actually a good idea.

Essentially, I remain convinced that any shaping I might do to malleable materials during construction would be all too easily overwhelmed by the many stresses of wearing the finished garment. As a result, steam-shaping of any kind has not made it into my pants technique, much as I like the romance of bringing forgotten techniques back to life. But I encourage you to explore this method if it attracts you. Please report your results to the rest of us! Sandra Betzina is the only contemporary sewing writer I know of who has written about shaping pants during construction. Her book *Power Sewing Step-by-Step* (Taunton Press, 2002) has some interesting suggestions.

**FOR THE MODERNIST:
A MINIMALLY SHAPED BACK**

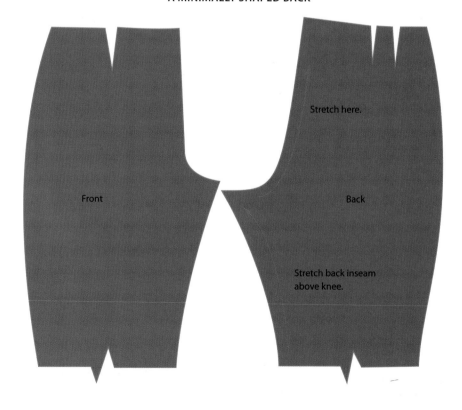

FELLING

Felling, shown in the photo and the top drawing at right, is a hand stitch used to secure a folded edge to another piece of fabric. It is typically used at the waistband to secure the band finish to the top edge of the pants, and none of it, of course, should ever be visible on the outside of the band.

The needle always passes only into the back layers (the band, say), going through just the inside of this layer and coming out through all layers. The exposed thread on the inside should be perpendicular to the stitched-down edge—and almost invisible when skillfully done in a matching thread. These visible stitches should be $1/8$ to $1/4$ inch (3 to 6 mm) apart and no more than $1/8$ inch (3 mm) long. I've convinced myself that stitching at the outer limits of these dimensions actually looks good, which is useful, because that's the easiest way to do it.

Felling is the only hand stitch that I use on a regular basis. You can watch my technique (such as it is) on the companion DVD-ROM.

BACKSTITCHING

Backstitching is the tailor's term for the most basic hand-made seaming and top-stitching stitch. This is the stitch that was used to hold fabric together before there were sewing machines. Stanley Hostek explains that variations in the backstitch's spacing, thread size, length of stitch visible on the garment face, and tightness allow it to be used, in skilled hands, for everything from bold saddle stitching to nearly invisible hand picking. Back stitching is part of both the pick (or prick) stitch and the hand-made bar tack, applied so beautifully in the tour's vintage garments.

Tiny, tightly packed, and hidden back stitches are the working part of the venerable bar tack. The visible part of the tack is nothing but a decorative covering. Hostek describes the visible stitching as two long stitches taken end to end over the backstitching and self-wrapped several times, by simply looping the remaining thread around the

Custom-made band linings are sometimes completely inserted by hand.

HAND STITCHES USED BY CUSTOM TAILORS

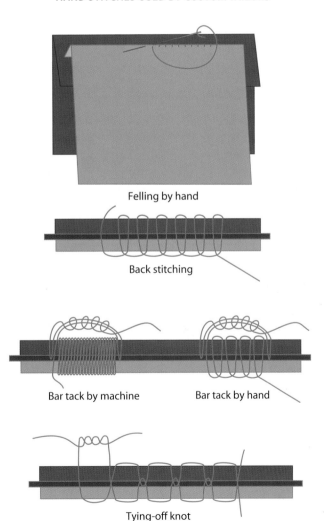

Felling by hand

Back stitching

Bar tack by machine   Bar tack by hand

Tying-off knot

long stitched ones, using the blunt end of the needle to poke the thread through, then backstitching once or twice to secure. The concealed working part of the bar tack could effectively be machine-stitched, as shown in the left-hand example within the drawing on page 119.

TYING-OFF KNOT

Whenever you're pulling threads to one side to tie them off, try wrapping the threads around one another two or three times, rather than once, as you'd normally do when making a basic square knot. When you pull this knot tight, it'll bind onto itself snugly rather than slipping loose while you wrap the second time—and then it won't matter as much if you make a true square knot on top.

READY-MADE WAISTBAND FINISHES

Tailoring suppliers usually offer some variety of preassembled waistband innards, combining a stabilizing inner piece with a multipart outer wrapping of bias fabrics—and sometimes a textured insert intended to keep shirt-tails tucked in (doesn't work). The folded edge is the lower edge, simulating an inserted curtain.

Just in case you've succumbed to the temptation of buying some of this ready-made waistbanding, here's how to use it. Either before or after you stitch the waistband fabric to the trousers, join the top edge of the waistband to just the outer open edge of the ready-made, right sides together, with a ¼-inch (6 mm) seam allowance, as shown in the photo below at left.

Press the seam open from the right side. Then fold the waistband over the stiffener layer of the ready-made, as shown in the photo below at right. Secure the ready-made from the outside as you would any finish, by topstitching, ditch-stitching, and/or attaching belt loops. The fabric pieces in the ready-made are all bias-cut, but only the lower, folded edge needs to be. The rubberized insert is decidedly optional.

The top edges of a band piece and a ready-made waistband are stitched right sides together.

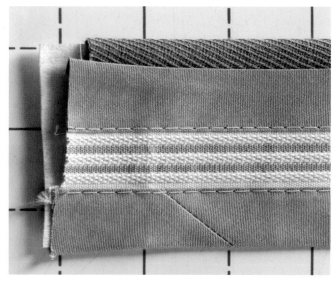

The band fabric is folded over the waistband layers.

AFTERTHOUGHT PLEAT STAYS

Here's a standard, sensible method found in sewing patterns for cutting front pants pockets that support pleats: Cut the front pockets out of two layers; the outer layer extends to the fly seams as an underlining to keep the pleats in front from spreading under any crosswise strain when worn. Not wanting to tamper with my well-loved, front-pocket techniques and not having made many pleated pants, I've developed my own solution to the spreading-pleat problem.

To keep pants pleats draping the way I envision them, I decided simply to build in a hooked strap that would work on the same principle: Let the pockets bear the strain across the waist (or just below it) so the pleats can hang free. With two doubled lengths of petersham and a hook-and-eye set, I was in business. I assembled and attached them as shown in the photo and drawing at right.

This simple add-on works just as intended, and I like the way the joined straps feel. This method transfers most of the circumferential tension from the waist to the hips. I prefer being able to put such a stay in after the pants are finished, when I can evaluate at my leisure whether I need a stay and where—rather than committing myself to a stay that's integrated into the pocket and fly construction and won't be easy to adjust later.

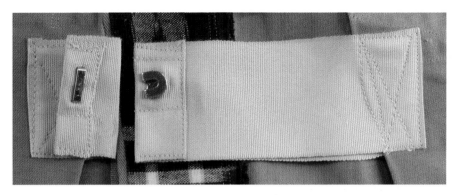

Petersham and a clamp-on hook-and-eye make a useful belt. Joined to front pocket edges, the belt makes a good pleat stay.

POSITIONING THE PLEAT STAY

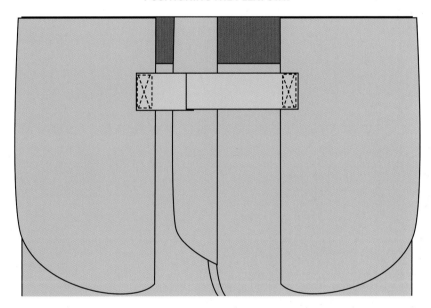

Place the stay just below the waistband and secure it through both layers of pocketing.

CHAPTER EIGHT

LEARNING FROM PROJECTS

Here's a quick tour of several of my most recent pants projects. In these photos, you'll see many of the techniques I describe in the book and how they work together within individual garments. You'll also find lots of variations on those techniques as I explore and experiment with them—and my conclusions as to what works and what doesn't, and why. For more photos of these projects and variations, see the Project Garment Galleries pages on the companion DVD-ROM. Ideally, you'll have the DVD open to these garment sections as you read this chapter.

CASUAL COTTON PANTS

I made these simple garments to test the fit of the pants I'd copied—one for me, and one for my wife. I'd been thinking about no-belt, no-back-pocket, button-fly, minimally structured, knocking-about sporty pants made from shirt-weight fabrics, with shaped slant pockets and buttoned waist closures—similar to elastic-waisted pull-on sports and leisure pants, but with a working front opening and no elastic. Here was my chance to try out these ideas. In addition to the lightweight fabrics, the pockets were the most interesting element to me. I decided to play a bit with exposing the pocketing a little, as faux piping, because I was using pocketing fabrics that contrasted nicely with the garment fabric.

WOMEN'S CASUAL PANTS

The front on my wife's pair of pants, shown below, is a cut-on band. It's got a sewn-on back band for variation's sake and because I thought the plaid would look interesting if it switched to horizontal there. When I started, I hadn't planned on letting the pocketing show along the pocket-mouth edge, but as I was turning it to the wrong side, I thought, "What a shame to hide this!" So, I started playing. A narrow roll of visible pocketing was easy to achieve, and it wasn't difficult to manipulate the extra width back out of sight at the top. I like it. I'll explore this one more! It's interesting (and annoying) that the vertical stripes on the pocket facings match the fronts when the garment is flat on a table, but not when worn.

Women's casual pants: These pants are made from shirting-weight fabric. They have a button fly and self-piped slant pockets, a cut-on front band, and an add-on, folded-over back band.

Two fly buttons are plenty for a 5-inch (12.7 cm) opening (not counting the band portion). I reinforced the band areas in front of the pockets with folded-double pieces of petersham intended to support and stabilize the button and the buttonhole at center front. I was afraid that the garment fabric alone would distort under the tension of wearing. The extra support works well to keep the band from looking strained, but it makes the buttonhole a bit stiff—not the most elegant solution imaginable. No doubt I could have gotten away with a single layer of petersham.

The self-fabric, button-strip lining is interfaced with a lightweight fusible. It is secured with a vertical line of topstitching just inside the fly opening, starting at the top of the petersham and ending a few stitches short of the bar tack at the bottom. Note that the

pocket bags extend to the top of the band, where they are hand-felled to the pants top to provide the band lining in their area. The hand-felling continues vertically down the bag edges at the side seams across the bands, securing and covering the side-seam ends of the back bands.

In back, the band pieces are simply folded to the wrong side over the top to provide a self-lining. The lower edge of the lining side is cut on the selvage, which extends far enough below the band/garment seam to cover the pressed-open seam allowances there. I interfaced the outer face of the bands with a lightweight fusible, not extending the interfacing into the allowances. After attaching the bands, I stitched the band layers together in the ditch of the pressed-open seam, first inserting a small piece of petersham between the layers at the center back as a stabilizing

layer. This insert also catches the bar tacks that I made at the top and bottom, to reinforce the vertical seam across the bands. Note that I decided not to allow any outlets (extra width) on the allowances at side seams, inseams, or centers.

MEN'S CASUAL PANTS

For my test pair, I wanted an even more pared-down, smooth look, so I chose to have no visible outside details except the contrast finish on the slant-pocket mouth and the two buttons at center front. I avoided any visible topstitching except at the fly. The bands are cut-on, obviously, and the fly is buttoned, hopefully not as obviously. For a detailed look at creating the pocket-mouth bindings, watch the videos on the companion DVD-ROM.

With the garment flat, you can perhaps see that the pocket openings end about ½ inch (1.3 cm) before they reach the side seams, unlike the women's casual pocket openings that end in the side seam (another variation detailed in the videos). This pocket-opening variation is a subtle difference, but a nice one, I think.

On the inside, these trousers are basically the same as the women's casual pants—with hand-stitched finishing at the top of the pockets and petersham band linings elsewhere. The differences are that I added outlets on the center-back and rear side-seam allowances and only backed the buttons (not the buttonholes) with extra petersham (which seems to have worked out

The front pockets line the front band where they can; petersham inserts fill in.

well enough, although I could have used a shorter extra piece). The whole idea of these petersham add-ons is less than ideal; I should have considered the reinforcement they provide and incorporated them into the design of the fronts more unobtrusively—but that's what happens with prototype designs: Everything's a test!

In the center photo at right, you can see how I've stitched vertically across the petersham and the pocket bag here and there to secure the waist structure as invisibly as possible. The striped fabric quite perfectly conceals these stitches on the outside. I also overlapped the rear petersham pieces at center back, underneath the bar tacks that reinforce the seam for added strength. These zigzagged tacks are actually easy to remove—a single snip with a fine-tipped scissors is all it takes—should I decide later to alter the waist circumference.

Men's casual pants: This garment has no visible details except the waist buttons and self-bound pocket mouths (shown below).

Occasional vertical lines of stitching at the pocket tops secure the petersham invisibly, in place of horizontal topstitching or belt loops.

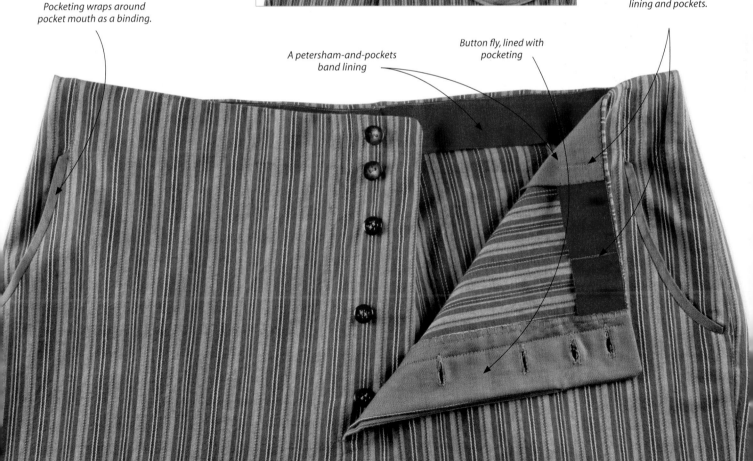

Pocketing wraps around pocket mouth as a binding.

A petersham-and-pockets band lining

Button fly, lined with pocketing

Vertical stitching secures the band lining and pockets.

DRESSY WOOLEN TROUSERS

These pants are my take on classic, wear-to-work woolen trousers, with belt loops, nylon-zipper flies, clamp-on hook-and-eye closures, and both welt and slash pockets. The waist linings are petersham, and the pocketings and fly linings are cotton shirting. Throughout I tried to keep the techniques here as traditional and as quick to do as possible, while including at least a few refinements or details (notably their curved pocket mouths) to keep the garments from seeming ordinary. Both projects started with classic commercial pants patterns, from which I took only the main front and back pant pieces and to which I added all my own details.

WOMEN'S DRESSY WOOLEN TROUSERS

Contrasting and slightly curved welt front pockets are the focus of these twill pants. The cut-on bands aren't noticeable when a belt of any sort is in place; but, as always, they simplify construction. I enjoyed adding a playful touch at the center back, with a doubled, chevron-shaped belt loop, echoing the angles of the little gap I left at the top of the center-back seam, adding "spring," as described in the custom tour (see page 25).

I've avoided any horizontal topstitching at the waist—and pretty much anywhere else, too. The belt-loop stitching serves very well to secure both the petersham and the pocket tops. I guess I should practice doing a nice-enough pick stitch so I can eliminate even the zipper topstitching!

Inside the fly, you can see that I finished the upper ends of the zipper tapes by folding them under as I stitched them down. On the underlap side, I also folded the tape in half lengthwise and stitched it to a fly extension, rather than adding a separate fly-shield piece. It's a type-B zipper (see page 79). The garment fabric is sufficiently lofty to conceal any

Women's dressy woolen trousers: These pants have cut-on bands, curved single-welt pockets, and a type-B zipper fly. A petersham band lining covers the pocket bags.

Belt loops secure the band lining, eliminating the need for topstitching at band. The center-back loop is doubled and spread into a V (see page 113).

Overlapping the petersham ends at the center back before securing the loop there reinforces the back waist.

bumps that this fold might otherwise create. Note that the overlap front edge is a fold, not a seam, as the facing there is a cut-on extension, too.

In back, note the single bar tack at center back, reinforcing the seam at the waist. The doubled loop is secured at the bottom with a few straight stitches vertically across the inside part of the folded loop-tube (visible in the bottom photo on the facing page). Note that here, as in the front, I positioned belt loops over darts. On the side, I concealed the vertical topstitching that secures the pocket bags by stitching it in the ditch of the side seam.

Inside, I overlapped the petersham ends at center back before stitching down the belt loops there. I like the extra strength this overlap seems to add.

The pocket bags are cut so the edges that cover the side seams are selvages. So, unlike the fly-shield lining, the edges don't have to be folded under before being topstitched in place.

I ran the petersham all the way around the band, covering the pocket tops, in the typical way. The main thing to note about the petersham is that I didn't stretch the lower edge before attaching it, so it doesn't match the garment circumference below the band portion of the pants. This difference causes some slight buckling of the garment layer just inside it, which is quite noticeable in these flat shots, but virtually disappears when worn. Minor as the problem is here, I won't leave out that step again.

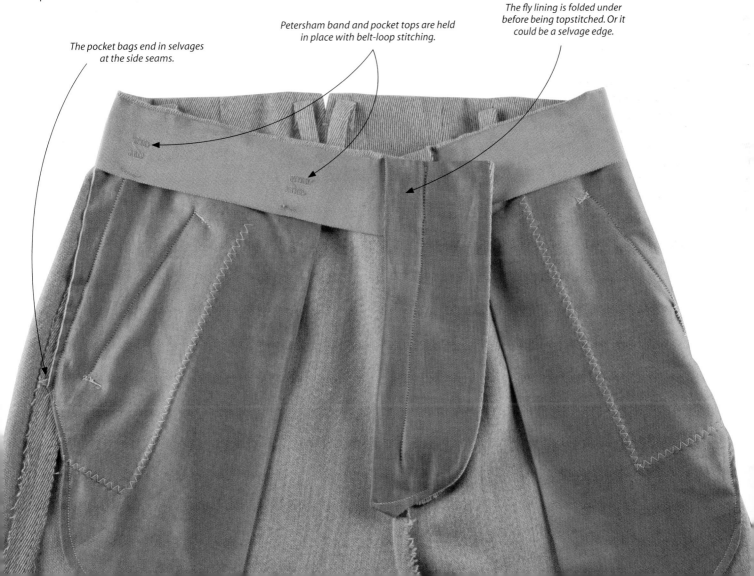

The pocket bags end in selvages at the side seams.

Petersham band and pocket tops are held in place with belt-loop stitching.

The fly lining is folded under before being topstitched. Or it could be a selvage edge.

MEN'S DRESSY WOOLEN TROUSERS

The main features in these trousers are the bands that appear in the front only, inspired by the Oxxford pants in the ready-to-wear tour (see page 20). The bands simplify the finishing of the pocket-mouth openings and the zipper tapes: They can all be covered at once with the applied band, rather than finished one by one, as with a cut-on band. There's a trade-off, though, because adding the band is more complicated than cutting it on.

The band/garment seam allowances are pressed open except at the fly, where I let the allowances turn toward the band, again for simplicity's sake. You'll see a different result in the men's garment on page 131. Similarly, I caught the zipper, teeth and all, in the fly topstitching, to demonstrate the lumps that result at the stitching at the base of the fly.

As on the women's trousers, I let the petersham band lining cover the entire band, including the pocket tops. I also let the belt-loop stitching secure the lining and the pockets, in lieu of any horizontal topstitching around the band—except for the few inches (half-dozen centimeters) of in-the-ditch stitching necessary at the front edges above the zipper to secure the outer band fabric as it wraps to the inside.

In back, the button loop at the welt pocket is the exact same structure as the doubled belt loop at center back on the women's pants on page 126. A turned belt-loop tube, folded in half to form a point and two parallel sides (in this case, tacked together to form a buttonhole substitute), eliminates the risky business of cutting a hole below the finished pocket mouth. I also concealed the side-seam topstitching that secures the pocket bag inside by stitching in the ditch.

Inside the fly, note the fork stays at the front crotch and the underlap fly extension that has not been cut away, visible to the right of the fly lining. I left the extension untrimmed as an experiment: Would I even notice it from the outside of the garment?

The extension seems to act as a kind of graded allowance between the fly structure and the outer fabric, but that's subtle and debatable. It's not too late to trim the extension away, even now; it's fused lightly right to its edges, so it needs no further edge finishing. I'll leave it for a while, until I'm inspired to remove it. I like the way it reminds me that there's no right way to do much of anything when you're making things for yourself.

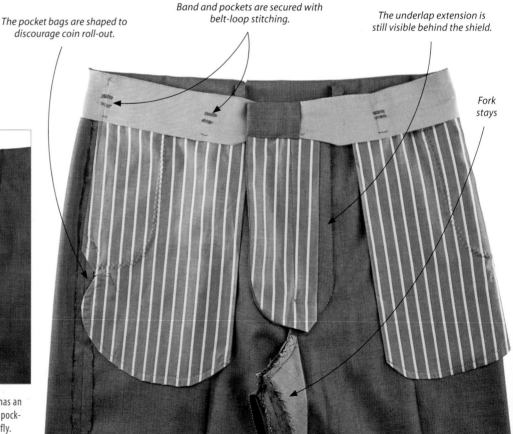

The pocket bags are shaped to discourage coin roll-out.

Band and pockets are secured with belt-loop stitching.

The underlap extension is still visible behind the shield.

Fork stays

Men's dressy woolen trousers: This garment has an add-on band in front, cut-on band in back, slant pockets, one single welt in back, and a type-A zipper fly.

EXPERIMENTAL DESIGNS

These last two garments are each the result of my noticing details online as I cruised images of current ready-to-wear and custom-made garments. The women's garment, made from a light-gray linen, comes from an afternoon's browsing at a major retailer's web showcase of designer women's pants for the Fall 2008 season. The men's garment, made from a sturdy cotton with a nice woven texture, was inspired by comments in a thread about adjustable-waistband solutions from custom tailors that I found on a popular men's dressing online forum. I used the tested patterns from the men's and women's casual cotton garments in this gallery as my starting points.

WOMEN'S SHAPED-BAND EXPERIMENT

For these pants, I was inspired by the dropped-waist, wide-band, big-tab look of the present (or just recently passed) day.

Never having made anything similar, I just dove in, with a wild notion about using large bias strips of silk as band linings-cum-curtains and a willingness to adjust to whatever issues came up.

The pants would have longish, low-set, on-seam pockets. They'd also have a short zipper with a dual hook-and-eye, plus internal button closure. I'd press all seams open to be as flat and unobtrusive as possible—my main departure from the examples that inspired me, which seemed to feature lumpy, exaggeratedly obvious construction despite their high cost, as if an essential part of the style was a reference to cheap ready to wear. That part I wasn't interested in.

On the outside of these pants, note the smooth, flat seam where the band joins the pants (evidence of carefully pressed-open band seams), the extended waist tab, and the on-seam pocket mouths. The main features are mostly hidden. Inside the fly, there's an inward-facing button and no obvious match-

ing buttonhole. The button is inserted into the band/fly seam opposite (the construction is thoroughly detailed in the video clips on the companion DVD-ROM).

The vertical edge of the band extension is a fold, not a seam. The seam joining the tab facing has been offset about $1/4$ inch (6 mm) inside the fold to keep the folded edge as straight and flat as it would have been if the facing had been cut on and not seamed on.

Inside out, these pants reveal the results of my experiment involving the bias band lining. I cut these lining pieces almost twice as wide as the bands, then stabilized them in the exact shape of their respective band pieces with a very lightweight interfacing. I cut the interfacing so as not to stretch around the circumference of the waist, leaving the seam allowances and the lower edges without interfacing.

After I attached the interfaced bands and completed the vertical pants seams, I folded the wide lower edges underneath the lining,

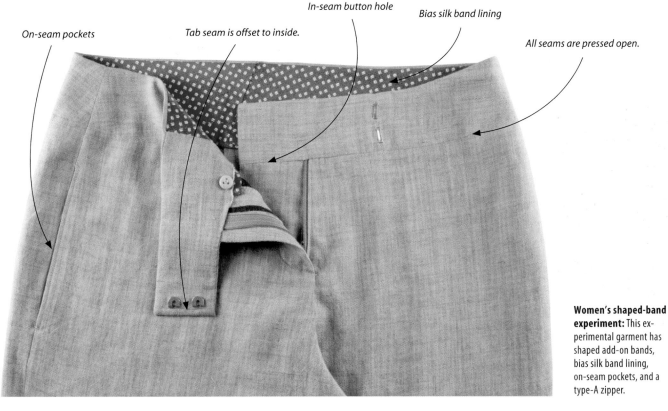

On-seam pockets

Tab seam is offset to inside.

In-seam button hole

Bias silk band lining

All seams are pressed open.

Women's shaped-band experiment: This experimental garment has shaped add-on bands, bias silk band lining, on-seam pockets, and a type-A zipper.

basting as I smoothed ripples out of the bias fold and letting the fold cover the pressed-open band/garment seam allowances. I did not stabilize this portion of the lining because I wanted its bias flexibility below the band and wanted the fold to be as soft and flat as possible. After completing the fly/band-facing assemblies, I backstitched in the ditch of the band/garment seam by hand to secure the lining all around.

The tracks of one of my unplanned experiments are revealed in the exposed black interfacing at the fly, visible in the photo on page 129. As I was preparing to attach the overlap zipper tape to the cut-on extension, I hit on a way to ensure that there would be no zipper or underlap imprinting on the fronts (I was concerned because the fabric was

proving less substantial than I'd anticipated). I decided to insert a zipper-length scrap of interfaced garment fabric under the overlap side's tape, to match exactly the depth of the folded-under underlap extension where the other side of the zipper was inserted. It worked perfectly to smooth all zipper bumps. It didn't occur to me, however, that I could conceal the interfaced side of this extra fabric simply by extending the right-side portion all the way out to the edge of the overlap facing itself. Oh, well. Next time.

The extra-wide fly shield grew out of my decision to put a buttonhole in the band/shield seam. The shield's partial lining was another spur-of-the-moment experiment. My thought was to extend the pocket-bag fabric edging I was going to use to bind the shield's

raw edge into something a bit more decorative. So, I made the edging much wider and stitched to the middle of the shield before folding it around the raw edge. I don't hate the result, but it seems a bit superfluous now.

I hand-stitched the lower edge of the band extension closed, as I recommend for band extensions with clamp-on hooks (see page 106). I also stitched the side-seam edge of the pocket bags (cut on the selvage) to the rear side-seam allowance, rather than through the whole garment at the side seam. The outlet at the rear side-seam made this easy to do. Finally, I hand-felled all the vertical edges where the band lining meets itself or the band facings, as demonstrated on the companion DVD-ROM.

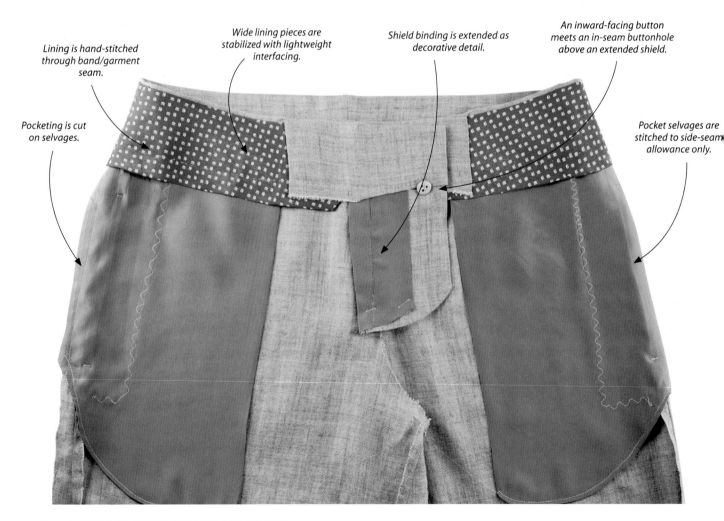

Lining is hand-stitched through band/garment seam.

Wide lining pieces are stabilized with lightweight interfacing.

Shield binding is extended as decorative detail.

An inward-facing button meets an in-seam buttonhole above an extended shield.

Pocketing is cut on selvages.

Pocket selvages are stitched to side-seam allowance only.

MEN'S ADJUSTABLE-WAIST EXPERIMENT

The experiment here was to see if I could extend an attached front band into tabs at the side seams, leaving the gap there between this band and the cut-on bands in back (as on pants I saw online made by the highly regarded Italian pants-maker Salvatore Ambrosi). You can see similar side tabs in the 1932 vintage men's pants on pages 24–25, although the Ambrosi pants are unattached at the side seams behind the tab—which seemed to me why they were flexible enough to snug up so unobtrusively when buttoning to a smaller waist circumference. The bands behind the vintage tabs are securely joined. (See the companion DVD-ROM to follow my steps for achieving these results.)

The pockets are shaped slants, ending in seams both above and below the mouth before reaching the adjacent pattern pieces (the bands at the top, the backs at the side). I added narrow pleats in front and a solitary single-welt pocket in back. Finally, I went to the extra effort of pressing open the band/garment seam allowances all the way to the center fronts and into the inside of the zipper structures for a much smoother, sleeker finish than I achieved on the woolen trousers, as shown in the photos on the DVD.

There are no belt loops on these pants, so I needed a way to secure the band-lining petersham strips on the inside. I settled on a single, unbroken line of topstitching that starts with the fly topstitching, turns 90 degrees just below the front band/garment seam, and continues across the side seam to the center back. In addition to the stitching around the pockets, this line of stitching is the only visible topstitching on the garment. As before, the pocket bags inside are secured with in-the-ditch stitches at the side seams.

The underlap zipper tape is type B, folded in half vertically and stitched directly to a cut-on fly extension. As usual, the overlap front edge is a fold, not a seam. The tab buttonholes are keyholes made with an eyelet attachment. The tabs are lined with the same petersham that faces the bands, pressed into shape and hand-felled to the pressed tabs, which were formed around a mildly stiffening piece of fusible. The tabs' allowances were basted into place with tiny strips of sheer fusible in preparation, like the shaped belt loop on page 112.

Inside, the pocketing and fly-lining fabrics are shirting cotton. Note the slight ripples along the lower edges of the petersham, indicating that it has been slightly stretched along these edges to keep them from binding against the below-waist garment shaping (lesson learned!). I cut outlets onto the side seams on the back pieces, more to mimic quality garments than for noticeable results. I had the fabric, so why not? Similarly, I extended the fly-shield lining to create a crotch-seam reinforcing tab above the fork stays I'd inserted. Customized! It's why it's fun!

Men's adjustable-waist experiment: This experimental garment has an add-on band in front with adjustable tabs at the side seam, cut-on bands in back, front bands that are not joined to the back, shaped slant pockets, one single welt in back, a type-B zipper fly, and front band/garment seams pressed open, even over the fly.

The pocket bags are shaped to keep coins from falling out. The petersham band linings cover the pocket bags and face the tab extensions. The shield lining is extended over the crotch seam allowances.

SOURCES

I've organized these sources by specific products—but each of these vendors offers many more useful items than the ones that I've featured here.

Assorted tailoring supplies

Atlanta Thread & Supply
695 Red Oak Road
Stockbridge, GA 30281
800-847-1001
sales@atlantathread.com
www.atlantathread.com

Banasch's
3380 Red Bank Road
Cincinnati, OH 45227
513-731-2040, 800-543-0355
bobc@banaschs.com
www.banaschs.com

Greenberg & Hammer Inc.
535 Eighth Avenue, 6th Floor North
New York, NY 10018-2446
212-246-2835, 2836, 2467, 800-955-5135
greenberghammer1@cs.com
www.greenberg-hammer.com

22L pants fly buttons

Bergen Tailors & Cleaners Supply Corp
9021 Old River Road
North Bergen, NJ 07047
201-943-4128, 800-932-4128
Information1@bergentailorsupply.com
www.bergentailorsupply.com

#40 basting thread, white, 2 oz.

B. Black & Sons
548 South Los Angeles Street
Los Angeles, CA 90013
213-624-9451, 800-433-1546
info@BblackAndSons.com
www.bblackandsons.com

15mm buttonhole cutter set; Chakoner chalk wheel; extra-fine fusing tape; interfacing; Kai embroidery scissors; point presser/clapper

Cutting Line Designs
1667 Barcelona Way
Winter Park, Florida 32789
877-734-5818
louise@fabriccollections.com
http://www.fabriccollections.com/

Tailoring board

Heirlooms Forever
3112 Cliff Gookin Boulevard
Tupelo, MS 38801
800-840-4275
www.sews.com

2-inch (5.1 cm) petersham

Judith M
104 S. Detroit Street
LaGrange, IN 46761-1806
260-499-4407, 877-499-4407
info@judithm.com
www.judithm.com

Interfacing; large, medium, and small clappers; pressing DVD entitled Fearless Pressing

Material Things
60–101 Parkside Drive
Port Moody, BC V3H 4W6
604-469-6953
orders@ceceliapodolak.com
www.ceceliapodolak.com

Interfacing; pants-fitting books and DVDs

Palmer-Pletsch Publishing
1801 NW Upshur Street, Suite 100
Portland, OR 97209
info@palmerpletsch.com
www.palmerpletsch.com

Seam Stick by Belva Barrick

The Sewing Place
4591 Longley Lane, #18
Reno, NV 89502
775-853-2207
info@thesewingplace.com
www.thesewingplace.com

Buttonhole cutter set; clamp-on hook-and-eye tape; Hug Snug rayon seam binding; #2 nickel-plated pant zippers

Sew True
447 West 36th Street
New York, NY 10018
800-SEW-TRUE (739-8783) or 212-239-0414
www.sewtrue.com

Dry iron

The Vermont Country Store
802-362-8460
customerservice@vermontcountrystore.com
www.VermontCountryStore.com

Clapper and point presser

Waechter's Silk Shop
94 Charlotte Street
Asheville, NC 28801
828-252-2131
info@waechters.com
www.fabricsandbuttons.com

FURTHER READING

The books here are listed in order of importance to me, rather than alphabetically. Don't be put off by the fact that all, except one of the Cabrera/Meyers books, are ostensibly about men's tailoring.

THE ESSENTIALS

These four books have been, for me, the most useful: *Men's Custom Tailored Pants* and *Hand Stitches for the Fine Custom Tailored Garment* by Stanley Hostek; and *Classic Tailoring Techniques: A Construction Guide for Women's Wear* and *Classic Tailoring Techniques: A Construction Guide for Men's Wear* by Roberto Cabrera and Patricia Flaherty Meyers. Anybody who is really interested in tailoring should at least have read them. As of this writing, they're all still in print.

Stanley Hostek's books, on pants and hand stitches, are from his set of four, the others being *Men's Custom Tailored Coats* and *Men's Custom Tailored Vests*. Except for the hand-stitches book, they're exclusively about men's wear, although there's much in all of them to interest any serious sewer. There's no information on fitting in any of Stanley's books, but he does still offer custom pattern drafting for men's suits, based on a questionnaire.

These are self-published treasures of the first order. Get them while you can, from Judy Barlup at www.uniquetechniques.com or from Stanley at:

Stanley Hostek
4003 West Armour
Seattle, WA 98199
(206) 283-6512

The Cabrera/Meyers books, published by Fairchild Publications, are exemplary, too, and are a little easier to follow than Stanley's books. His are more like extensive pattern instructions, needing to be read step by step. The Cabrera/Meyers books are both more extensive and considerably less detailed, covering multiple garments and topics. There's a lot of duplication between the men's and women's versions. If you can get just one, I'd recommend the women's volume, regardless of which gender you're sewing for, simply because almost everything in the men's book is in here, too, along with a lot of fascinating material that's not in the men's book (like how to add pleats and make a wider variety of pockets, just to mention the pants-related stuff). Both books cover fitting and construction.

CURIOSITIES

The rest of the books I mention here have functioned more as curiosities than essentials for me—meaning that I treasure my copies, but can't promise that the modern sewer will find much of real use in them, except for the tacking ideas in the J. E. Liberty book. I list them simply because you won't see them elsewhere, and you might enjoy tracking one or more of them down before they vanish forever. All are out of print, so your best bet is to do an interlibrary-loan search for any of these that seem interesting to you.

Practical Tailoring, by J. E. Liberty, Pitman Publishing, London, England (1933, 1947, 1960)
This is the old tailoring book I mentioned a few times; fascinating diagrams, but if you can easily make heads or tails out of the jargon-filled text, you're either a time-traveler or were raised in an English tailor's workshop!

The Art of Garment Making, by either Phillip Dellafera or Archibald A. Whife, Tailor & Cutter Limited, London, England (1952, 1967, respectively)
The Whife book claims to be a revision and re-authoring of the Dellafera. The contents are substantially different, but equally vintage, especially regarding pants. If you want to learn about riding breeches, plus-fours, split falls, etc., in addition to classic vintage dress trousers, these are your books.

Tailoring Suits The Professional Way, by Clarence Poulin, Chas. A. Bennett, Company, Peoria, IL (1953, 1973)
Written in the 1950s, this book includes several drafts for men's and women's garments along with step-by-step directions for moderately high-quality construction of basic suits. I wish I had the older edition; the last one has been updated and has lost some interesting material in the process.

How to Make Men's Clothes, by Jane Rhinehart, Doubleday & Company, Garden City, NY (1975)
This one contains lots of excellent introductory chat for home sewers interested in the tools and tricks of men's tailors. It also includes a men's pants draft and way too sparsely illustrated step-by-step directions.

The Art of Sewing: Basic Tailoring, Time-Life Books, NY (1974)
From a vast set of lavishly produced sewing and crafts books by this publisher, this volume is totally focused on the craft of custom clothing, mostly for men. It features a long and detailed treatment of making dress pants, but I found it confusingly illustrated and difficult to follow, even though it's in modern English and the illustrations are abundant! But perhaps there's some gold in there—I can't tell. Maybe you'll be able to?

PATTERN INSTRUCTION SHEET

The instruction sheet for Claire Shaeffer's Vogue Pattern #7468 is excellent, offering both couture and ready-to-wear techniques, and much more detail overall than most pattern instructions, for Yves Saint Laurent-inspired trousers, similar to those discussed on page 15.

MAGAZINE ARTICLES

Many issues of *Threads* magazine have articles pertinent to pants making. Here are several I've especially earmarked:

"Lining Pants," by Connie Long; September 1998, Issue #78
This article covers full and partial pant linings, so I don't have to. Thanks, Connie! ***Connie's Easy Guide to Sewing Linings*** (Taunton Press, 1998), is also excellent.

"Pants-Pattern Upgrade," by Mary Ellen Flury, March 1998, Issue #75
This article offers detailed, step-by-step instructions for making the trousers shown on page 17. (1998 was a good year for pants in *Threads*!)

"The Petersham Waistband," by Sandra Betzina; May 1998, Issue #76
This article focuses on skirts, but covers petersham in detail. It's worth plundering for minimalist trouser waistband ideas, too.

ABOUT THE AUTHOR

David Page Coffin, a former editor at *Threads* magazine, is the author of *Shirtmaking: Developing Skills for Fine Sewing* (Taunton Press, 1998). He has conducted sewing and tailoring workshops throughout the United States, Canada, and the United Kingdom.

David has been a frequent guest host on several online sewing forums and has hosted live chats on PatternReview.com. He has appeared on Sandra Betzina's HGTV sewing program, and his instructional videos have been broadcast on YouTube.com and have received great reviews on ThreadBanger.com, PatternReview.com, and other sewing sites. David hosts http://myvirtualworkshop.blogspot.com and http://makingtrouserswithdpc.blogspot.com, David's blog all about making trousers and specifically designed for the readers of this book. He lives with his artist wife, Ellen, in Brookings, Oregon.

Painting: Ellen Coffin

CONTENTS OF COMPANION DVD-ROM

To view the enclosed companion DVD-ROM, you'll need a computer that has a DVD drive. The DVD-ROM contains several large PDF documents. You'll be able to view these with most PDF-viewing applications, but you'll only be able to watch the videos if you're using Adobe Reader to view them and also have the QuickTime video player from Apple installed on your computer. Both are available free for many versions of Windows and Macintosh operating systems. I recommend that you download the latest versions of both of these utilities before running the DVD-ROM on your computer.

To download Adobe Reader, visit www.adobe.com. To download QuickTime, visit www.apple.com. For a preview of the DVD and more details on how to use it, visit http://makingtrousersdvd.blogspot.com. You'll also find links to Adobe and Apple there, too.

BONUS CHAPTER: KEYHOLE BUTTONHOLES

Video Tutorials

Cutting Out Tips

Easing/Ripping Tips

Slant Pocket Variations 1

Slant Pocket Variations 2

Slant Pocket Variations 3

Piped Pocket

Side Pockets: Women's Experiment

Finishing Front Pockets:
    Men's Experiment

Welt Pocket: Men's Experiment

Button Fly 1

Button Fly 2

Button Fly: Men's Casual

Shortening Zippers:
    Men's Experiment

Zipper Fly: Men's Experiment

Zipper Fly: Women's Experiment

Hooks: Men's Experiment

Eyes: Men's Experiment

Hook-and-Eye Tip

Cut-On Front Bands: Men's Casual

Cut-On Back Bands: Men's Casual

Shaped Band 1: Women's Experiment

Shaped Band 2: Women's Experiment

Shaping Tabs: Men's Experiment

Tabbed Bands 1: Men's Experiment

Tabbed Bands 2: Men's Experiment

Tabbed Bands 3: Men's Experiment

Back Bands: Men's Experiment

Finishing: Men's Experiment

Adjustable Waists

Hemostat Tip

Sewing on a Button

Keyhole Buttonholes 1 & 2

RTW and Custom Garment Galleries

Project (Author's) Garment Galleries

Printable Patterns

Sources, Further Reading, and
    Extended Links

INDEX